CW01314851

First published in Great Britain in 2024
Copyright © Tommy Sampson 2024
Published by Victor Publishing - victorpublishing.co.uk

Tommy Sampson has asserted his right under the Copyright, Designs and Patents Act 1988 to be identified as the author of this work.

All rights reserved. No part of this publication may be reproduced, distributed, or transmitted in any form or by any means, including photocopying, recording, or other electronic or mechanical methods, without the prior written permission of the author.

Every reasonable effort has been made to trace copyright holders of material reproduced in this book, but if any have been inadvertently overlooked, the author would be glad to hear from them.

ISBN: 9798873861552

Victor
PUBLISHING
victorpublishing.co.uk

FROM THE DEN TO WEMBLEY

By
Tommy Sampson

FROM THE DEN TO WEMBLEY

"Success is never final.
Failure not fatal.
It's the courage to continue that counts"

Winston Churchill

FROM THE DEN TO WEMBLEY

FROM THE DEN TO WEMBLEY

CONTENTS

Acknowledgements & Dedications 9
Foreword - by Alan Walker 11
1. Growing Up 15
2. Into The Lions' Den 23
3. The Hard Work Starts Here! 31
4. Turning Pro 61
5. Dropping Down 65
6. Moving On 91
7. Bromley-bound 103
8. A New Challenge 109
9. A Good Deal 123
10. The Road to Wembley 129
11. What Happened Next? 203
The Last Word - by Steve Lovell 223
In Memoriam 225

ACKNOWLEDGEMENTS & DEDICATIONS

My wife Sandie for her patience and encouragement whilst I wrote this book; Steve Lovell - a great friend through difficult times ; Chris Bethell -Whom without his valuable contribution this book would never have made it to print; Billy Neil -who I am privileged to call my friend; John Flaherty, a fantastic guy who I have sadly outlived; Micky 'Ned' Kelly my respect for him knows no bounds; Theo Foley who played a huge part in my career; Derek Possee for looking after me when I was a kid; Derek Smethurst - my golfing partner and lifelong friend; Ronnie 'Butch' Howell - for giving me my first life lesson; Jack Burkett - A great professional ; Frank Saul - my hero; Barry Bridges who used to put his arm around me and offer me advice about how to defend against pace (flogging a dead horse comes to mind!); Alan Dorney, who always looked out for me; Keith Lissenden - A Loyal friend; Roy Smith, who made Wembley possible; Colin Ford, for being with me all the way; Terry Martin, my captain; Dave Wadhams who stood by me through the dark days.

FROM THE DEN TO WEMBLEY

FOREWORD
BY ALAN WALKER

I was delighted to be asked by my great friend Tommy Sampson to write the foreword for his book. I didn't realise just how similar and how many coincidences our careers, and ultimately our lives, have taken.

It's a story that takes you from growing up in south east London, joining Millwall Football club as a fifteen-year-old apprentice professional, and turning full professional to dropping down into non-league football, originally as a player, and then manager.

Progressing on to his greatest achievement winning the Carlsberg FA Vase in 2000, beating Western league side Chippenham Town 1-0 in front of over 20,000 fans.

Seven years after Wembley Tom suffered a massive stroke, leaving him with a mountain to climb and, to be fair, one that he is still climbing.

As I mentioned earlier, there have been some remarkable coincidences in our lives. For instance, we were both tough uncompromising defenders - although Tommy was a far better footballer than me - and played for The Lions.

Both of us played at and managed numerous non-league clubs around Kent and the south east. We also had the fantastic experience of winning at Wembley - me as a player, Tommy as a manager, which puts him in an elite group, as it's far harder to achieve as a manager than as a player.

Then on to our most difficult challenge yet. My accident where I broke my neck, then Tommy's stroke, which left us both with life-changing physical difficulties.

During the conversations we still have together it's glaringly obvious we are both still in love with the beautiful game!

When playing games against any of Tommy's teams, it was always hard. They were tough, very well organised, drilled and had a togetherness that was directly shaped by Tommy. He was always respectful and would shake hands and hug me regardless of the result, an attitude which comes through in abundance in this book.

With his physical issues he is still fighting his biggest battles but, as he always did, he is doing so with determination, sheer hard work, intelligence, and always with that amazing attitude of a born winner.

It's a fight I am very confident he will win.

Enjoy the book!

Alan Walker

FROM THE DEN TO WEMBLEY

1
GROWING UP

I was born to Maisie and Johnny Sampson at Guy's Hospital, London on the 18th August 1954. Dad was a wealthy man owning a meat haulage business.

He had around 20 lorries on the road at any one time delivering meat to all the major ports including Harwich, Dover and Liverpool. He would often drive a lorry himself when required. Mum was a housewife and semi professional singer sharing the bill with such luminaries of the time, Frankie Vaughan, Dickie Valentine and Dennis Lotus.

Dad was a very busy man, coming home at all hours. He had a huge yard at the Elephant and Castle which was about 300 yards from were we all lived, just off the Walworth Road. Occasionally I would spend a day with Dad whilst he did his deliveries around the country. I was probably only four or five at the time so climbing into the big bullnose truck was exciting for me as a young boy and, more importantly, got me off school for the day!

The family was growing. I had older siblings in Tony who was four and sister Lynn, seven. The three bedroom house that we lived in was shrinking fast! Mum was trying to persuade Dad to find a house befitting the size of the family and the need for a larger property became imperative when Mum fell pregnant in November 1956. We obviously did not have a television as Mum and Dad had to fill the time some how! So, when my younger brother Leigh arrived the following August, Dad's ears were bleeding with Mum's constant pleadings for a move to larger premises.

To be fair Dad did Mum proud buying a beautiful 3 bedroom detached house in Grove Park a suburb of Bromley, Kent. The house sat on the corner of a cul-de-sac facing the gates of Grove Park Hospital. Dad still kept the yard at the Elephant and Castle. Mum was overjoyed to be in a more than ample three bedroom house with a large garden and a huge garage. Dad was now driving a band new Jaguar with running boards and huge fenders. The year was 1959.

Mum's first task was to find schools for Lynn and Tony who were now 13 and 9 respectively. Lynn was placed in Coopers Lane Girls School, just around the corner. Tony however was accepted into the quaintly named Marvels Lane Junior School which was half a mile from home. The walk to school was a good forty minutes. In todays climate people would be horrified to let a boy of nine years old walk unaccompanied on sometimes dark mornings. Luckily, there were lots of boys that attended the same school and therefore Tony was never really alone because of the number of children walking the same route.

Mum was now working in a nearby florists in Eltham. She had the use of a dark blue transit van because as part of her job description was to drive to Covent Garden and pick up the fresh flowers daily at the crack of dawn. In those days Covent Garden was based near Vauxhall so she left at five each morning leaving Lynne to get us boys washed and dressed ready for school. Mum would arrive back just as we were leaving for school. We left her eating a slice of toast then she would leave for work.

I was now six and had joined the same school as Tony. Leigh, being only four, attended the Marvels Lane Nursery School. Tony was now in the fourth year waiting to take his eleven plus exam. He was captain of the school football team which by association made me feel a bit special. Tony passed his eleven plus exam and moved on to Mallory Secondary School, so Leigh and I were left behind. Leigh had gone through his nursery section and infant school whilst I was in the fourth year. My footballing prowess was starting to be noticed and now I was the captain of the school football team, following in Tony's footsteps.

The manager of the Blackheath schools under 14s district football team was a teacher from the area called Andrew Kurowski who would watch me play for the school team every Saturday morning. I was a centre-half in those days because I was taller than the rest. Heading the ball was my biggest asset. I was therefore delighted when, a few weeks into the new season, my school football team manager Mr Leonard Parkin informed me that I had been selected to play for the under 14s against East Kent Schools in a fortnight's time at the home of Southern League team Dover Athletic.

The year was now 1965. I was eleven and very dedicated to the point that I would clean my boots as soon as I had finished playing, polishing them until you could see your face in them!

Over the next few weeks I attended every district training session without fail. We trained mostly at the playing fields of a posh school called Blackheath and Blue Coats. I remember practising my heading for hours until the light faded.

One evening after training Mr Kurowski informed us we were to play East Kent Schools the following Saturday at Dover Athletic FC. We were to meet at Grove Park railway station at 11am. This was great for me as I could walk there from home in about ten minutes.

So, come Saturday morning, with boots gleaming and shin pads in my kit bag, I strolled up to the station were I met the mini bus being driven by Mr Kurowski. I took my seat with about seven of the team, the rest meeting us at Dover. Just over ninety minutes later we arrived at 'The Crabble', Dover Athletic's quaintly named stadium.

The football pitch was about 60 feet above us, so we all started to walk up this rickety old wooden staircase where, arriving at the top, we turned right towards our dressing room. It was a bitterly cold September morning and our dressing room offered us little or no warmth. Reluctantly we all started to get changed into our kit that Mr Kurowski was handing out from a moth-eaten old kit bag. I asked for the number six shirt, the same number my hero Bobby Moore wore for England and West Ham. Our captain was to be Ian Thorpe, my partner in the centre of our defence. Ian being left footed - and me particularly strong on my right side - meant we were perfectly matched.

We didn't have a formation in those days. We were still playing the old 'W' system which meant the full backs marked the two wingers and the centre-half marked the centre forward leaving the two half-backs winning the ball and trying to supply the two wingers. Ah, where did it all go so wrong?

At twelve I had cemented my place alongside Ian in the district team. The next two years saw us play lots of representative football, putting together a great run in the prestigious English Schools Trophy, reaching the quarter finals where we were drawn away to Plymouth Schools.

I had passed my eleven plus exam with flying colours and was accepted into my first choice secondary school: Roan Grammar School for boys, a posh prestigious school with a strong naval tradition. Luckily my defensive partner Ian also won his place at Roan Grammar. This was beneficial to us as we became such good friends and our football partnership in the district team blossomed.

FROM THE DEN TO WEMBLEY

It was now 1966 I was six months short of my thirteenth birthday playing for Blackheath Under 14s. Our game against Plymouth Schools was to be played immediately after a Plymouth Argyle first team game. Our opponents had this supposed 'wonder kid' called Trevor Francis who I was given the task of man marking.

The game finished 0-0 after extra time so I'd done my job to prevent him from scoring. The replay was to take place ten days later at Charlton Athletic's cavernous Valley stadium. I was up against Trevor again but this time the roles were reversed as I gave my team the lead with a thumping header from a corner.

Francis however had the last laugh, scoring his team's late winner to set up a tough fifth round tie against Waltham Forest, a team full of guys tied to West Ham United. If my memory serves me well, I think Forest prevailed.

FROM THE DEN TO WEMBLEY

Marvels Lane School Team with me as captain, holding the trophy

Trevor Francis (left) and Ian Thorpe shaking hands before the game, I'm standing at the back, fourth from the right.

FROM THE DEN TO WEMBLEY

Me wearing the number five shirt as Trevor Francis (number 10) scores a late winner for Plymouth schools.

FROM THE DEN TO WEMBLEY

2
INTO THE LIONS' DEN

It was around this time that I had a gaggle of scouts and club representatives badgering my mum and me, desperately trying to get me to put pen to paper to sign schoolboy forms for their club. Eddie Firmani the legendary Charlton Athletic manager visited us several times along with his youth team scout Les Gore.

Gore, like Millwall's legendary youth team scout Dickie Waterhouse, had followed my career from the age of twelve. I was now thirteen and still playing for the Blackheath District Under 14s. The offer from these clubs was to sign schoolboy forms which tied you to the club concerned from the age of twelve to fifteen. The only club to offer a financial inducement was Millwall, who offered £500 for my signature.

It was gradually coming down to a choice of Millwall and West Ham United. John Lyall - West Ham's assistant manager - and their hugely respected youth scout Wally St Pier made a very persuasive case for the east London club. Mum was at this time going through a very messy divorce from my Dad.

The decision to sign with Millwall was based purely on the journey to each club. Millwall was one bus from where I lived in Lee Green. West Ham was a train into London and then a tube to Upton Park. We were now in March 1966, four months away from England's World Cup triumph. I was twelve years of age and training two nights a week at The Den for which we were reimbursed our expenses.

Confession time! There were nights when Mum would drive me to New Cross bus garage where I would walk to the ground and still claim my expenses. Get in!

At this particular time there were loads of lads like me training two nights a week trying to earn a three year apprentice contract when we turned fifteen. All of these lads were in the same boat as me, having clubs from all over the south east vying for their signature. One of these lads was a great friend of mine Micky Kelly. Ned and I were good mates, having played together representing Kent and London schools. Mick and I were occasionally let off school to train with Millwall's first team. On these occasions we would meet at New Cross Gate railway station and pay a visit to the local greasy spoon to fill our bellies with a full English. Then we would walk the half mile to the ground were we would follow the players and jog to Deptford Park, where alongside a 400 yard cinder track was an enclosed full size football pitch.

The surface of this football pitch was loose shale on top of a concrete base. Ned and I lined up with all the other players - about 28 strong - to be split into four sides of seven, playing across the pitch. Once the teams were picked, manager Benny Fenton would blow the whistle and off we went. Benny usually put a condition on these games. On this occasion you were only allowed two touches, encouraging control and play. So we had two seven-a-side games going sideways across the top and lower side of the pitch.

At each end of these two pitches were two iron goals so, if you were lucky enough to have picked first team 'keeper Bryan King, he would go in goal. As for the other goal, it was whoever volunteered. Eat your heart out Pep!

This surface was brutal and impossible to turn on or stop. A pass not played perfectly would mean the ball being given away cheaply. I found these 'make it up as you go along' games very difficult. For the last couple of years I had been playing five-a-side on grass in studs, so I thought: what would I do in a normal game? I decided to attach myself to Ronnie 'Butch' Howell'. It didn't take me long to realise I had dropped a massive bollock!

I had got tight with Ronnie and forced him into a corner of the cage. He half turned around to me spitting through his teeth and said: "You little cunt! Do you know who I am? Fuck off back to your Mum!"

I was shocked at this tirade and gradually backed off to re-join the game. Ronnie was about 21 and thought he was the dog's wotsits! He was an unpopular bloke in the dressing room because of his lack of respect for the senior pros. I suppose this was my first taste of 'the mans' game.

I have to admit that night at home I was shaken, I was thirteen and my ego had taken a massive hit. Going back to boys football was refreshing, but the incident with Butch stayed with me for years. When I told Ned he laughed and said: "You have to grow up and look after yourself."

I looked up to Ned , despite me being a school year older than him. He was a great player and unlike me was built like a man. Along with all that he had an ego the size of Kent. I had eighteen months to prove I was worthy of a three year apprentice contract.

Those next 18 months saw me fulfil my obligations to training two nights a week at The Den. Because we weren't allowed on the pitch, these sessions were mostly stamina work, running on the shale track around the playing surface. Most of these sessions were taken by first year pro Alan Garner. Occasionally the Under 18s youth team manager Charlie Vaughan would turn up to cast an eye over this group of potential apprentice professionals. There was me, Micky Kelly, Bobby

Pittaway, Malcolm Hobbs, Malcolm Davies, Roy Compton, Alan Ballard, Steve Webb, Jonny Johnson, Andy Bushell and John Flaherty.

We were all great mates and on odd occasions Charlie would pick one of us to play in either the Under 17s or the Under 18s in a South East Counties game the following Saturday morning.

My first crack at playing at that level was an away game at The Hayes Stadium, west London, against Queens Park Rangers. I spent the whole ninety minutes chasing the future captain of the English national team Gerry Francis. After that experience I knew I needed to be fitter, leaner, and tougher if I was going to become a proper player!

During that final 18 months, along with Ian Thorpe and Micky Kelly, we played loads of representative football. Together we played in some very good schoolboy sides. Ian and I played in the Blackheath District side that went unbeaten for 18 months. Ned played for Woolwich and Kent schools. Being part of that undefeated run helped win me a schoolboy international trial at St Albans FC. The trial was split into two teams, the South East v South West. I played for the South East, in the South West team was Plymouth's Trevor Francis. Sadly, I failed to impress enough to make the final England squad to play Scotland the next summer at Wembley.

That was a massive disappointment for me but something I had to just deal with. I was almost fifteen and, as yet, had not experienced failure, so I had to find the strength to overcome that disappointment. That feeling was new and it really tested me. I had no father figure at home because Mum and Dad had divorced and Dad had left home.

I was still doing my two nights training every week at The Den. There was always lots of gossip after training.

"Who you are going to sign for?"

"Has your Mum and Dad been offered money to sign for someone?"

I am pretty sure there were a few porkies being told, as lads were quoting all sorts of figures off the top of their heads. I then casually said we have been offered ten thousand pounds by West Ham for my signature!

The other lads nearly choked.

I kept that lie going for weeks, I was constantly being interrogated about my claim until somehow it got out that I had signed schoolboy forms for Millwall. So all the guys were, like me, waiting on the club to make a decision as to whether to offer us apprentice contracts.

One training night in December 1968, Charlie Vaughan, our youth team manager, pulled John Flaherty and me aside to tell us that we would be signing three year apprenticeship deals on our 15th birthdays. As most of the lads were getting changed, Charlie pulled us aside into the upstairs tea room to give us advice on what to do now. He told us both what good players we were and under no circumstances to waste the opportunity we had been given.

He told us both that manager Benny Fenton was delighted to have us on board. We were both still to turn 15 and had our school year to finish. Charlie was never a man to show his emotions, although the big beaming smile he had on his face gave away how proud he was of both of us.

Most of the guys had changed and gone home. Charlie asked us not to tell any of the others as he wanted to tell them of their fate himself. John and I shook hands, hugged each other and excitedly left to walk the half mile to New Cross bus garage where we would both jump on buses for home. John and I were very close because we had been training together since we were twelve, striving to get that apprenticeship deal. Before I jumped on my bus I rang Mum to tell her of my good news. She told me wait and twenty minutes later pulled up at the bus garage in her two tone red roof and white body Ford Anglia and I jumped in the front seat beside her. I told her what Charlie had said and she told me how proud she was and that she would ring Dad and tell him the good news.

As we set off for home, I asked if we could stop off at The Den. The gates and players' entrance were still open. We parked up and went in. I led Mum through the corridors of the club's offices and down the stairs where, at the bottom we both walked towards the tunnel.

After twenty paces or so we were outside and onto the playing surface. As we both looked around at the stadium and pitch, I said to her:

"Just imagine watching me running out of the tunnel, making my debut in front of 12,000 people..."

Would it ever actually happen I wondered.

FROM THE DEN TO WEMBLEY

Eddie Firmani - Charlton Athletic's legendary manager and Italian international

Bryan King - First Team Goalkeeper

Ronnie Howell - Gave me my first life lesson!

Micky "Ned" Kelly - Big mate and super footballer

Alan Garner - First year Professional

Charlie Vaughan - Under 18s Youth Team Manager

FROM THE DEN TO WEMBLEY

Blackheath Under 14s - Ian Thorpe (Captain) holding the ball, I am on the front row, 2nd from the right.

3
THE HARD WORK STARTS HERE!

During that summer I was getting really excited about starting my career at Millwall but, at the same time, I was also very apprehensive because I couldn't forget the Ronnie Howell incident. Would it always be like that?

I got up early for my 'first day at work'. I was to catch a number 21 bus that would take me through Lewisham and up Loampit Vale and into New Cross where I would get off at New Cross Gate station to walk the half mile to the ground. I had done this walk a hundred times on those twice-a-week training nights, only this time it felt different. I was walking into a 'man's world'. When I got to the ground I looked up at the car park which was full of shiny cars, Ford Granadas and Capris. I allowed myself to wonder what it would be like to drive my own shiny new car into the club's car park. The silence was broken by someone shouting my name.

I turned around to see John Flaherty jogging towards me. It was great to see him, we were both starting our first day so I am sure it was a comfort for both of us. We walked into the home dressing room to report to first team physiotherapist Jack Blackman.

The dressing room was full of senior players getting changed into their first team kit. Jack was in his late fifties having been a bustling centre forward for Brentford and Queens Park Rangers. He introduced John and I to second year apprentice Pat Lally who would show us the ropes. Pat gave John and I some kit to put on and then we followed him down the tunnel onto the pitch where there were lots of photographers and guys with notebooks. This was the club's press open day. There were also a row of about 25 chairs where the players would sit in alphabetical order to be photographed and interviewed. I found my seat and immediately someone sat down next to me, he half turned and offered his hand, asking my name. I told him and he replied: "I'm Derek Possee". Over the next fifteen minutes Derek and I chatted, with him asking questions like: 'How old are you? 'What position do you play'. The conversation eased my nerves. Along with Keith Weller, Derek was one of the club's star men.

The chair to my left was filled by £35,000 summer signing from Chelsea, Derek Smethurst. Smethy and I were to become great friends and golfing partners, playing endless rounds over the next three years. Smethy and I were an odd couple. He was from Durban, South Africa and I was your stereotypical Cockney boy from the Elephant and Castle!

After a couple of hours of interviews and photographs Benny called us all into the dressing room. With everyone sat down, the Gaffer gave a pre-season pep talk as well as introducing new first team coach Andy Nelson. Andy had the gait of a guardsman and a big booming voice. He had been captain of Alf Ramsey's Ipswich team that won the First Division, stunning the football world in 1962 having just been promoted from Division Two. Since 1965 Andy had been running his playing days down in the west country at Plymouth Argyle.

Benny then introduced the new intake of first year apprentices: Tommy Sampson, John Flaherty, Malcolm Hobbs, Steve Webb, Roy Compton, Malcolm Davies, Johnny Johnson and lastly goalkeeper Alan Ballard.

Benny then turned to the second year apprentices in their final year to wish them luck before hopefully turning pro: Jimmy Godfrey, Pat Lally, Steve Brown, Dougie Alder, George Duck.

The first team was split into three different groups: the star men: Dennis Burnett, Keith Weller, Derek Possee, and then the veterans: Harry Cripps, John Gilcrist, Ken Jones, Billy Neil, Eamon Dunphy and Gordon Bolland. Then came the younger guys: Barry Kitchener, Alan Dorney and George Jacks. Alan had come through the junior ranks. George was a free transfer from QPR.

There were also new faces in Brian Nichols who had been signed from Fulham, as well as Barry Salvage from QPR. This left Harry Cripps looking over his shoulder at Nichols and Salvage who were both left-backs and possible replacements for him. Benny had also signed right-back Brian Brown on a free transfer from Chelsea which probably meant the end for veteran John Gilchrist. In addition, Benny had first year professional Alan Garner who was great cover for any defensive injuries.

The gaffer then pushed me and John Flaherty forward to be interviewed by veteran press hack Maurice Woolf. Woolf was chief sports reporter for the South East London Mercury. The idea was for John and I to wax lyrical about the club's youth system.

Once the formalities of the day were over, the gaffer gathered everyone around to announce the details of pre-season training which was to start tomorrow. The pros would meet at Greenwich Park, Blackheath at 10:30am in their training kit which Jack and Pat Lally had laid out for them, then the pros all went home. The first and second year apprentices all stayed behind to hear Jack dish out the tasks we would have to undertake on a daily basis.

I got the job of laying out the players' training kit every morning, a right cushy number compared to cleaning boots and mopping floors. I have to admit, after all these years. Never once did I clean a pair of boots (except my own!).

The following day all first year and second year apprentices - about twelve in all - clambered into the club dormobile to be driven to Greenwich Park with first team coach Andy Nelson at the wheel. In the back it was like "sardine city". I am sure the current day nit-pickers would throw their arms up in the air, quoting health and safety issues. But back then life in general was far more relaxed.

On reaching the park we got out by the tea and cake pavilion. The Gaffer was already there with several first teamers. We all got out and followed Andy and Benny down to the statue of General Woolfe who proudly overlooked the Maritime museum. I didn't know what to expect. So there we all stood in blazing sunshine looking down at the path that crossed the park just in front of the museum.

I knew the park very well as my old school Roan Grammar was right next to the park in Maze hill. The drop from the Woolfe statue was 600 feet (200 yards). The Gaffer paired us off. I was with John Flaherty. Right at the front Benny set me and John off with everyone behind us. The first bit of the run was all downhill so naively John and I set off at a good pace. Behind us 'Crippo' and 'Gilly' were shouting for us to slow down. Eventually John and I reached the bottom of the hill and, as per Benny's instructions, turned right across the bottom of the park before reaching the other side at the bottom of Maze Hill and again turning right to run up the other side of the park, another 600 feet straight up. No wonder the more experienced players were telling us to slow down!

John and I looked at each other and as we were leading the whole group we felt we had to give the last 600 feet our best shot. We were absolutely cream crackered but with first team coach Andy Nelson impressively at thirty five years of age running right behind us, we felt the pressure on us to keep up the pace. Looking upwards towards the top of the hill I could see the Gaffer standing there. I nudged John to let him know who was watching. The next thing I remember was Andy's big booming voice encouraging John and I to give the last forty yards everything we had. We took off as fast as we could before collapsing together, almost at the Gaffer's feet.

It was already very hot and all I could think was: *if this was only the first session of the day, what would this afternoon bring?* We were scheduled to go to our training base near Mottingham. When everybody had finished the run we walked across the top of the park back to the pavilion where all the cars were parked. Benny got into his and told everyone to follow him to our training base. It was now about 11:15, so, with the sound of car doors slamming, us apprentices climbed back into the club dormobile.

Pulling out of the park we followed the procession of cars behind Benny. I knew our training base because I only lived down the road at Lee Green. It was a beautifully-appointed training facility owned by the biscuit company Peak Freans, with eight changing rooms and four tarmac tennis courts. There were four football pitches and a small cricket pitch. The pitches on the top half of the field were used by amateur players at the weekend. The football pitch we were going to use was behind an eight foot hedge at the bottom of the field. After the morning training session, everyone took a bit of time to relax in the blazing sunshine.

Opposite the gates of our base was a large pub called The Dutch House. This is where we were all going to have lunch, but before we could get there, we had to navigate our way over the very busy A20 dual carriageway. Once across we went into the main hall attached to the pub. Andy and Benny were already sat down, probably discussing the afternoon session. We were allowed a large glass of orange juice and a selection of cold meats. Once us apprentices had finished our meal, Benny called me and John over to let us know what equipment we would need for the afternoon session.

We had brought with us two sacks full of balls, bibs and cones. So after navigating the A20 again we would go and organise the equipment the Gaffer had requested. The heat was incredibly intense so with only about forty minutes to go before we started again we all laid down to try and enjoy the sunshine. The apprentices always stuck close together, we were very close friends through all those twice-a-week training nights. It was difficult to stay awake, the heat was so oppressive and then, breaking the silence, we heard the booming voice of Andy Nelson ordering not just us but all the senior pros down to the bottom pitch for the afternoon session.

Everyone was still exhausted from the morning's exertions. The apprentices were debating what the afternoon session was going to bring. Benny was a very forward-thinking manager for that era. We all assembled at the bottom half of the field, apprentices and senior players alike, and he split us up into pairs all with one ball.

I teamed up with John. One of the pair would serve up a ball for his partner to head back. Firstly we would be ten yards away from each other, then gradually we would get further apart. After the heading we would move on to sidefoot volleys. We were now a good fifteen yards apart and then it would be chest control and full volley back to your partner.

This went on for about 30 minutes. The heat was up around 30 degrees and gradually we all got further and further away with each skillset becoming more and more difficult. At 30 yards apart one partner would be asked to hit a pass to his mate who would control the ball on his thigh. At the end of this skills session we would split up into maybe four teams of six and play against each other. The morning's running had taken its toll on the group because these small sided games were a poor excuse for competitive games of football.

With everyone showering and drying off, the pros were able to head home. All the apprentices climbed into the dormobile once more, to be driven back to The Den. Tantalisingly for me, Andy drove right past my front door in Lee Green where I lived with my mum and elder brother Tony, but it would be a little while before I was actually back home because I had my apprentice tasks to finish back at the ground.

When Andy got us back to the ground I went straight to Jack who was down in the cellar where all the pipeworks were. I had to help Jack pack the training kit for tomorrow. When the baskets were full of kit, they were checked and packed. I then said goodbye to Jack to make my way up to the bus garage and jump on a number 21 bus for home. I was absolutely shattered when the bus pulled up at Lee Green. I jumped off to walk the couple of hundred yards to my home, the heat was unrelenting and that walk home seemed to take forever as my legs felt so heavy.

Looking back on my first day as a professional footballer, I could only think about Ned who was still attending school because he couldn't start as an apprentice until next summer. My first day had me believing I really was a proper footballer. It was only a few weeks previously I had been kicking a tennis ball around in the playground with my mates.

When I got home Mum was very excited to hear about my first day, Tony, my brother, was less than indifferent to hear what I had to say to Mum. Tony was a milkman and had been home since noon having finished his round.

I phoned Ned to tell him how my first day went. After having had my tea I slumped into an armchair to read the newspaper. It wasn't long before I fell asleep only for Mum to wake me up to watch Coronation Street (yes I know that sounds sad!) but those were the times we lived in. I could barely keep my eyes open for the rest of the evening. You couldn't record anything in those days, so reluctantly I took myself off to bed at about 8:30pm, missing Z Cars. To this day I have never felt that tired again. I realised that there was a lot of growing up for me to do both physically and mentally.

Pre-season lasted three weeks with every day following exactly the same format. When we finally finished and got back to the Den it was a bit of a let down. Peek Freans was such a beautiful setting, The Den was a harsh reality. All of us apprentices were gradually settling in and becoming part of the fabric of the club and those nerves that we all felt on the first day were slowly dissipating.

The first year apprentices were all working alongside the second year ones who were in their final year before learning if they would sign full professional contracts. All of the first year apprentices were 17, whilst my group were mostly about to turn fifteen. The club were obligated to fulfil pre-season friendly matches against non league-sides. No first team players were to be involved in these games because of the risk of injury so, close to the season starting, that meant it was left to the apprentices to make up the numbers in these games.

I remember going to play Essex Senior League team South Ockenden United. This was where the club first spotted Pat Lally before they signed him on as an amateur player. Pat was now one of those second year apprentices playing against his old club. Andy Nelson had the somewhat dubious honour of taking charge of the team. The game was a reward for our opponents because of Pat. Ockenden would normally play in front of 100 or so fans but that night that figure probably trebled and therefore bring much needed finances into the club.

It was exciting getting changed into the first team kit for the first time. South Ockenden's facilities were spartan to say the least, but the floodlights were good. We set up in a 5-3-2 formation with me playing sweeper behind central defenders Alan Garner and John Flaherty. The three midfielders that night were Jimmy Godfrey central, Douggie Allder left side and Steve Webb right side with George Duck up front alongside Roy Compton. George was technically gifted, his first touch under pressure was outstanding but his Achilles heel was his lack of pace (sorry George!) Roy on the other hand was young and for his age very strong and good in the air.

We won the game fairly comfortably as you would expect. I had never played in that formation before so I had to think on my feet. That was my first game as a professional footballer and considering all things I was pleased with myself.

I was soon brought down to earth when the coach dropped us all off at the Den and John and I had to walk to New Cross bus terminal to each jump on a bus to get home. Sitting on that number 21 bus I was thinking about what it would be like to play for the first team in front of 12,000 people. Tomorrow it would be back in the same old routine: number 21 bus to New Cross, walk to the ground, lay out the training kit for the senior pros, jog to Deptford Park, pick sides, play two seven-a-side games until about midday, jog back to the ground, shower and go home.

It was around this time first team player Gordon Bolland, who lived just up the road from me in Blackheath, asked me where I lived and offered me a lift home. So from then on Gordon took me home after training for months. He was 27 and I was two weeks short of my fifteenth birthday.

I wasn't supposed to start my apprenticeship until I was fifteen, but the club turned a blind eye. Gordon had joined the club the previous March. He drove a beautiful Ford Granada and despite the twelve year age gap we got on famously.

He offered to pick me up every morning but I had to decline his kind offer because I had to be in the ground for 9am to sort the players' training kit out whilst Gordon didn't need to be in until 10. So until I passed my driving test, it was a bus to New Cross then walk to the ground to sort the kit out, but at least I would get a lift home everyday.

Bolland had enjoyed a varied career. He played for Leyton Orient, Chelsea, Norwich City and Charlton Athletic before joining Millwall. He was a midfield player who liked to get forward and nick the odd goal. He was the first team's regular penalty taker and if my memory serves me well, I don't think I ever saw him miss one.

It was getting close to the season starting. The Saturday after the South Ockenden friendly the same side went to play Bexley United of the Southern League. It was a blazing hot afternoon. Bexley were a big, strong physical team, something I had not come up against yet. Another part of growing up I suppose. Although it was a Saturday the first team were in training. For this friendly Charlie Vaughan was in charge. We drew the game 2-2 in front of about 500 people and arrived back at The Den around 6pm. The first team were long gone so it was back on the number 21 bus for me to get home.

FROM THE DEN TO WEMBLEY

Monday morning came around and again yes, you guessed it right, a number 21 bus and a walk down Brocklehurst Road to Cold Blow Lane, sort the training kit again then when everybody was ready, another jog to Deptford Park, pick four teams of seven and play across the top of the pitch while in the lower half of the pitch Benny was in the middle of the two games trying to referee both. It was absolute chaos at times. I absolutely hated Deptford Park and the type of 'training' we did.

The only respite was playing reserve games.

The reserve team played in the Midweek League which was made up of teams like Luton, Watford, Aldershot, Northampton, Brighton, Leyton Orient, Peterborough, Charlton, Southend and Cambridge. Despite being first team coach, Andy Nelson was give the onerous task of taking charge of the reserve team.

This was OK as long as the game was at home. If we were away on a Tuesday evening to somewhere like Peterborough it was a different kettle of fish. I think Andy felt these duties weren't on his job description when he first came to the club. To be fair Andy was a true professional and he just got on with it. I Liked him. He had played for Alf Ramsey which was good enough for me. He had also been a great defender playing centre half for the lpswich team that won the first Division in 1962. He would often put his arm around me and offer me his advice about different aspects of defending.

During that first 69/70 season the reserve team was mostly filled by those first and second year apprentices. It was very rare for genuine first team players to appear in the 'Rezzies'.

On odd occasions fringe players like Billy Neil would play as well as trialists from non-league clubs. I remember players like Peter Hawkes (Fisher Athletic) Peter Mcgillicuddy (Leatherhead) Billy Holmes (Woking) Robin Wainwright (Hitchin Town) Gordon Hill (Southall) Trevor Pearce (Malden Vale).

FROM THE DEN TO WEMBLEY

It was soul destroying playing reserve team matches on a Tuesday afternoon at The Den in front of twelve supporters not the 12,000 I had envisaged that day when Mum and I had walked out of the tunnel when I first signed my apprentice contract.

How did I know it was 12 people? Well I had plenty of time to count them!

I only remember one of those reserve games and that was one afternoon at The Den when playing Southend and this hunched-shouldered guy humiliated me in the space of about fifteen yards nutmegging me and then dumping me on my arse as I tried to show him down the line.

His name? Oh yeah it's coming back to me: Peter Taylor. Whatever happened to him?

Days like that made me tell myself I was not going down without a fight. Along with reserve team matches, us first year apprentices would play under 17s South East Counties League football against fellow under 17s opponents from Crystal Palace, Tottenham, Watford, West Ham, Fulham, Ipswich and Arsenal. Being captain of that side meant over the years I shook hands with many players who went on to become legends of their clubs.

The likes of Wilf Rostron (Watford) Jimmy Cannon (Crystal Palace) Kevin Lock (West Ham) Liam Brady (Arsenal) Les Strong (Fulham) Ray Wilkins (Chelsea) Steve Perryman (Tottenham) and Kevin Beattie (Ipswich). Of all these players I was closest to Ray Wilkins and Kevin Beattie. We would often chat on the phone on the Friday night before each of us played.

We played our home games at Eden Park Avenue in Beckenham which belonged to British Rail and the playing surface was always in pristine condition. After playing at The Den in Midweek League games on a bumpy surface it was a joy to get to Beckenham. Those times playing under 17s football were the best times I had in my days at the club. At various times Charlie would promote one of us to the under 18s and I distinctly remember me and John Flaherty being selected to play Tottenham under 18s at their training ground in Cheshunt, north London. I played in midfield whilst John played left back. I was in midfield for one purpose only and that was to man-mark Graeme Souness.

Souness had already made his first team debut for Spurs so I was under no illusion as to how difficult this was going to be. So, as per Charlie's instructions, every time he was on the ball I was within touching distance. He soon got wind of this tactic and looked at me saying: "Fuck off back to south London!".

To be honest he was just too good for me, but I stuck at it and I realised I was getting under his skin. I thought: 'What can I do to really piss him off?' Then it came to me. I decided that every time I got close to him I would call him "Jock". So he received the ball and I said: "Careful Jock, I'm right behind you". Again he told me to fuck off. I replied: "Is that all you've got 'Hamish'?".

All these years later I have to confess he was super-talented and far too good for me. In midfield with me that day was second year apprentice Jimmy godfrey. Jim couldn't stop giggling at me because I think he must have thought 'fair play to the lad, he's obviously got some balls'. Souness shook my hand at the end of the game, looked at me and said something I will never forget: "Leave your name and address in reception and I will send you a photograph of the ball". Charlie gave me a big hug in the dressing room before acknowledging mine and John's performances. I was on cloud nine being driven home by Charlie. He dropped me at the New Cross bus garage where I jumped back on that number 21 bus home.

Gradually during that 69/70 season I settled in to my role as a central defender, playing just off of my centre half. I played lots of reserve games with first year professional Alan Garner as my centre-half. He would attack the ball while I would drop off and cover. I was 5 foot 8 inches weighing 10 stone 4lb, my lack of height wasn't a problem because of my ability to read the game. I never understood why the reserve team weren't asked to set up the same way as the first team. I always felt that this would make it easier for any reserve team player having to deputise for one of the first team to adapt.

I started to become a deep thinker about the strategy and tactics of the game. I was convinced that when my playing career was over I would become a coach or manager. I was only fifteen and thinking like a 35 year old. That was typical of me, a very old head on young shoulders. One of my proudest moments was the night the reserves were playing away at Watford when Andy Nelson told me to lead the team out as captain. Despite it only being a meaningless reserve team match, I was bursting with pride. Here I was, just fifteen and captain of Millwall's reserve team alongside being captain of the under 17s South East Counties youth team.

I felt that my leadership qualities were being recognised. I thrived on organising everyone. I was always very vocal and treated every game I played in as a cup final. Those dreadfully depressing nights away to Peterborough were to me the biggest game imaginable. It would be my voice barking out orders, piercing the deathly silence. There may have only been less than 20 people watching, but to me there was 10,000. My enthusiasm and ego wouldn't let me believe it was a nothing game. In the back of my mind I was playing for my life. Who knew who could be watching? Whoever that person was, I was determined to impress.

I spent my whole footballing life waiting for a pat on the back which to me meant I had done well. I needed that because it was my reward for having given everything. I never left anything on the pitch. It never occurred to me not to give everything I had.

Those training days at Deptford Park were virtually worthless, the surface as I have said was impossible. All of us apprentices were constantly being slaughtered by the senior players for making mistakes. It would have been easy to have hidden but I made a point of getting fully involved in those seven-a-side games as I wanted people to know I was prepared to make a mistake to earn their respect.

I vividly remember the day having finished training, I got back to the ground and found one of the other first year apprentices sobbing in the boot room because of the unrelenting criticism he had received during the session. I tried consoling him but he just couldn't stop crying. I felt so sorry for him because he was a good friend of mine.

I went home that night thinking of my friend and how he must be feeling. The following morning I was sorting out the training kit for the players when Benny came into the dressing room and asked for the rods to be taken to the park. The rods were three feet long metal poles which Benny would hammer into the surface. This meant we would be running all morning, doing 'doggies'.

The rods would be hammered into the surface at ten yard intervals and you would set off in fours, going to the first one and back then the second one and back and so on.

The relief on my friend's face was obvious because this meant there would be no seven-a-side games and he wouldn't have to face the barrage of criticism he had suffered yesterday.

We spoke quietly in the corner of the boot room and I said: "That's a touch." he smiled.

I couldn't get his predicament out of my head because our job was to play football and he was relieved that we weren't going to play games which I found really sad. The stick given out by the senior players was brutal and vicious sometimes but I saw it as part of growing up. I was lucky because it never happened to me. The only person I got abuse from was Ned, he had high standards and if he thought I wasn't meeting them I'd get an earful. The second year apprentices were all fighting for that first year contract.

Jimmy Godfrey was a great lad and looked after us young guys. Then there was Dougie Allder. Everyone was pretty sure he'd sign pro and then probably walk into the first team which he did. Doug had a great attitude and was a solid bloke. I liked him. When I played under 18s football he was always supportive and full of encouragement. Then there was George Duck, who had great ability and again was a thoroughly nice guy who went on to have a stellar non-league career. George scored goals for fun all around the non-league scene. After joining Southend from Millwall George went to Wealdstone where he scored an unprecedented 251 goals in 370 appearances. He is still a legend at Wealdstone but his real claim to fame was scoring the first goal for Dagenham in the 1979/80 FA Trophy final where they beat Northern League side Mossley at the original Wembley Stadium.

Pat Lally, a tough hardnut when he played, was another cert to sign pro. Lastly, there was Steve Brown. Me and Browny never really got on. He had wonderful ball skills and again a dot on the cards to sign full pro. He had a very sarcastic nature and we would both have a pop at each other every now and again. I think he felt I was Charlie Vaughan's pet project. I still believe that to this day. He felt that I had to be knocked off of my pedestal. When we see each other now and again we are best buddies!

That first season saw the first team start with only three points from their first seven games. Everybody was walking on egg shells around the Gaffer. During that time there were a number of Monday morning inquests. Apprentices were ordered to the bootroom, with the door firmly shut, supposedly out of earshot, but you couldn't fail to hear what was being said because of the raised voices. It was uncomfortable listening at times with accusations flying back and forth. These inquests could last over an hour at times. Andy Nelson would sometimes have to intervene as it got really heated and personal.

At last, after eight games, the gloom lifted when Carlisle were put to the sword 4-2 at home with Weller and Bolland both getting a brace. The atmosphere in the dressing room lifted instantly. As a young fifteen year old I was thinking these "bare your soul" meetings could easily do more harm than good. The intensity of those inquests were frightening.

Before the turn of the year Benny added three more players to the squad, all with a West Ham connection. Firstly goalkeeper Jim Standen and then left-back Jack Burkett and lastly forward Brian Dear. All three were part of the West Ham United team that won the Cup Winners Cup at Wembley four years earlier. Standen was a part time cricketer playing County cricket for Worcestershire. He was a more-than-competent deputy for first team 'keeper Bryan King who had been the subject of rumours about moving to a First Division club. Standen, despite only being cover for 'Kingy', was the consummate professional. The way he trained was a testament to the standards he had set himself during his illustrious career.

Burkett was exactly the same. He turned up to training immaculately dressed every day, bang on time. I admired him because whenever he had to play reserve team football he accepted it graciously. He helped me enormously. I would hang on to his every word, and despite me still being only fifteen, he accepted me barking out orders.

Playing with the likes of Burkett and Standen elevated my view of myself. I felt my maturity was showing itself loud and proud. As for Brian Dear, unfortunately I cannot speak about him in the same way.

He was a foul-mouthed individual who disrespected Jack Blackman on a daily basis. He would walk into the bootroom where we were all sat on the bench and would lash a ball at us just for the fun of it. You can only imagine how pleased we all were when we heard he had gone back to West Ham having managed only four appearances in the first team.

He was without doubt the most obnoxious guy I ever met during my short tenure as a professional footballer and in my humble 31-year career in the non-league world.

The high point of that season was to see Pat Lally make his full debut at home to Cardiff City - John Toshack and all.

By the end of the 69/70 season, Dougie Allder and Steve Brown had signed full professional contracts and had made their first team debuts. Also in the club were trialists Billy Holmes and Dave Coxhill. Billy was a front player whilst Dave a midfielder. All through that season there had been a lot of noise around Keith Weller leaving the club for big money.

Keith was a fantastic footballer and would be almost impossible to replace. He and Derek Possee were a potent strike force. The season had just finished when the inevitable happened and the club accepted a fee of £100,000 from Division One Chelsea. Unfortunately for me, my last interaction with Keith was to sell him my 12s/6d FA Cup Final ticket for the upcoming Chelsea versus Leeds final. At the start of the following pre-season I was hauled into the secretary's office to be told my ticket had been found in the hands of a well-known tout on the day of the final. This put me in deep shit!

Somehow this news found it's way into the national papers and the following publicity was unpleasant for both me and the club. As you can well imagine I was the butt of incessant stick from the first team dressing room. "Kingy" would shout at the top of his voice: "Here he comes Tommy the tout!"

I had to wait all through that pre-season for the Football Association to determine my punishment. I wouldn't have minded but Keith only gave me £4 for the bloody ticket and what were the chances of my ticket being found out of the 100.000 people that attended the game?

Our pre-season preparations were exactly the same as last season's. On a brighter note I had been joined in the apprentice ranks by big mates Ned Kelly and Bobby Pittaway. The sad thing for me was that Andy Nelson had left the club to manage Gillingham. His replacement as first team coach was former Lions' keeper and proud Scotsman Lawrie Leslie. This appointment didn't go down well with the dressing room and looking back I believe this was because Lawrie's expertise was as only as a goalkeeper and not a coach.

Lawrie was a lovely man but having finished a disappointing tenth last season, the senior players had no confidence in him. Nelson was such an impressive man with a bit of swagger and Lawrie just couldn't fill Andy's shoes. Having Ned and Bob around was great. We had known each other for a number of years. Mick was a silky midfield player whilst Bob was a ball-playing dominant centre-half.

Meanwhile Benny was still searching for Weller's replacement. He managed to pull a big rabbit out of the hat by signing QPR's ex-Chelsea and England international 28-year-old Barry Bridges. The plan was to pair him and Derek Possee up front as a lightening-quick front two. That didn't necessarily mean a long-ball tactic, because in our midfield we had clever footballers in Gordon Bolland and Eamon Dunphy who could thread passes through to Derek and Barry.

When 'Bridgo' arrived he took a shine to me and would often put his arm round me and talk to me about defending against pace. When we played first team v the reserves in training it was your worst nightmare defending against Derek and Barry. I know many of you Millwall supporters of a certain age will remember 'Poss' and 'Bridgo' with the same fondness that I do. Watching Barry train made such an impression on me. He never gave anything less than his all.

When the manager put the first-team sheet up on a Friday lunchtime he often included one of us apprentices to travel with the team, essentially to help Jack with the kit. If we were at home it was a great experience to be in the dressing room and listen to the Gaffer give his team talk. At fifteen I remember travelling overnight to Middlesbrough. I roomed with Gordon Bolland and I felt that I was finally a bona fide professional footballer.

I was captain of the reserves on a regular basis as well as captain of the south east counties under 17s youth team. I was 18 months into my apprenticeship and growing in confidence. As I have said before, every game I played was, in my eyes, a cup final.

Talking of cup finals, I finally received the result of the Football Association's enquiry into my ticket misdemeanour. Benny called me into his office to show me the letter the club had received from the FA.

Their findings were that I was to be banned for five years from receiving a Cup Final ticket. I thought: *fair enough, no harm done.* It could have been worse, there could have been a large fine to pay. Benny had made it clear to me that the club would not pay any fine I might be given.

After about three months of the season the first team were lying just below halfway in the league. Derek and Barry had six goals apiece. Gordon Bolland had also chipped in with four of his own. He giving me a lift home every day was very much part of my learning curve, despite him being twelve years my senior we chatted on equal terms.

I felt I was maturing as every week passed. Living on £7 per week wasn't easy, so I had to borrow off of Mum and Tony if I wanted to go out. My girlfriend Linda lived in Camberwell so that was two buses from where I lived in Lee Green. When I got there we would walk along the Walworth Road to the Temple Bar pub, have a quick drink and then I would walk her home for a snog in her doorway. Then, for me, another bus home through Peckham and Lewisham.

Buying a second hand car was out of the question and learning to drive was also not an option because I was still only fifteen. Most mornings on the way to work I would meet Ned and he would stand me breakfast. Even to this day we still joke about how much in debt I am to him for those breakfasts, but in truth, I actually owe him more for being a great friend.

We were just coming to the turn of the year and the first team had turned it around, sitting just in the top half of the table. I now had just eight months or so to show the Gaffer I was worthy of a professional contract. John Flaherty and I were almost exactly the same age - being four months between us - this meant he would know his fate before me. We had done all those training nights together and were still almost neck-and-neck in the race to our footballing destiny.

George Duck and Pat Lally had joined Steve and Dougie as contract professionals. Sadly Jimmy Godfrey had missed out. The first team finally finished tenth and 70/71 was to become my second full year as an apprentice.

Jack awarded me the title of senior apprentice or S.A.P for short. Dougie was now a first team regular whilst Browny was mostly a sub. Dougie had no airs and graces, he was always just a regular bloke. After finishing playing a South East Counties game on a Saturday morning, the apprentices would jump on a train at Eden Park railway station to Waterloo and then back to New Cross to walk to the ground and watch the first team play.

We watched the game from just to the right at the end of the players' tunnel in front of the shed where Roy the groundsman kept all of his equipment. On a regular rota basis two apprentices would go in the dressing room when the game finished to pick up the kit and sweep the floors. On the rare occasion that we had lost, going in the dressing room could be tricky especially when there was a 'discussion' going on.

Just like those Monday morning inquests it could be heated. Benny on occasions like this would tell the two apprentices to go forth and multiply. That heated discussion would resume on Monday morning. I always felt that straight after a game was a bad time to hold an inquest into what had just happened because emotions were very raw and it would be too easy to say something you would regret.

I once saw Benny lose it after an away defeat. Players would be hurling accusations at one another and it was particularly unpleasant. Back at the hotel where we were staying the then first team coach Andy Nelson pulled me aside and told me quietly not to tell anyone of what I had heard or seen that day. Sheepishly I said "OK".

FROM THE DEN TO WEMBLEY

At the start of the 70/71 season Derek Smethurst cut a forlorn figure. Since he had signed the previous season he hadn't had a sniff of first team football. We got chatting and he used to ask me the best way into the ground from where he was living in New Malden. I knew Dougie Allder lived that way so I told him to ask him. Anyway it turned out that Doug would pick Smethy up every day. Through that we became friends. We shared a passion for golf and talked about playing together one day.

It was difficult because I didn't drive and with Smethy getting a lift in with Dougie we were both left at the ground after training without a car or clubs. This would all change when I passed my driving test the following September.

The 70/71 season started disastrously with only one win from their first five games. That win came courtesy of a Derek Possee hat-trick in a 3-1 away win at local rivals Charlton. Because of that start it was eggshells around the Gaffer time again.

The Possee/Bridges partnership was still bedding in. By Christmas the duo had scored 14 goals between them with Harry Cripps and Barry Kitchener nicking the odd goal here and there so by the turn of the year the pressure was off.

Smethy still hadn't had a sniff of first-team action so he was in and out of Benny's office more times than a fiddler's elbow on a busy night. He told me that when he signed, Benny assured him of a first-team spot. His mood was always low from then on.

Daily training at Deptford park didn't help. Another player getting frustrated with his situation was my central defensive partner in the reserves Alan Garner, who left for fellow Division Two team Luton Town where, in 73/74, he led them to promotion to Division One.

Also leaving that summer was first year professional. Pat Lally leaving for Fourth Division York City. With Dorney and Kitchener fixtures in the Gaffer's team I could understand the logic in their thinking.

With Alan leaving this meant that my partner at centre half in the reserves would be fellow-apprentice and great friend Bobby Pittaway. Bob and I played against some legends of the English game. Ex-Spurs man Bobby Smith was winding his career down at Brighton and Hove Albion. Similarly ex-Ipswich and England international Ray Crawford at Colchester United. I felt that

I was getting closer to becoming someone who could perhaps deputise for almost any number of players in the first team barring the front two. I was convinced I could deputise for Dennis Burnett at a moment's notice. I would not take my eyes off of Dennis when watching the first team play in his position playing as a sweeper behind Alan and Kitch. I used to think it would suit me down to the ground. I didn't need to be 6 feet 3 inches or super quick, I just needed to read it right. Which was a strength of mine.

I didn't say any of this out loud because I didn't want people to think I was getting above myself. Ned however was the opposite of me. He would quite openly state his case for a midfield berth and he would eventually get that chance.

The 70/71 season was a disappointing one for the first team, finishing eighth. Possee and Bridges managed only 13 goals between them. Dougie Allder was becoming a fan favourite playing every game bar two. His work rate and all action style saw him lauded by the Millwall faithful. It was very frustrating for Steve Brown who spent the majority of the season sitting on the bench. It appeared that the Gaffer didn't have the same faith in Steve as he had in Dougie.

Smethy again cut a lonely figure as he didn't get one opportunity to play. As for me it was the same diet of Midweek League and youth team football. Our daily training routine never changed. Deptford Park and two teams of seven playing against each other on that poxy surface. Only very rarely did we get on the pitch and when we did it was a refreshing change.

First team coach Lawrie Leslie unfortunately was very limited and his ideas of how we should use this opportunity of training on grass didn't go down very well with the likes of Possee, Dunphy, Bolland and Cripps.

There was one occasion I remember vividly when Benny came out of the players' tunnel, looked at this shambolic session and immediately put a stop to it. Benny took over for the rest of the morning and at least everyone got a feel of the ball. It was embarrassing for Lawrie because his lack of imagination had been exposed brutally. Because of our training routines I was learning nothing, none of us apprentices were! It was a complete waste of time and the only time we learnt anything meaningful was through playing games.

I was lucky because people like Jack Burkett, Barry Bridges and Derek Possee would offer me great bits of advice which I took on board willingly. I owe those guys so much because they helped shape my playing career and improved my football knowledge.

With the season over, the apprentices under Billy Neil's stewardship were again about to undertake our series of odd jobs around the ground. Basically if it was stationery we painted it. Walls, floors, gates, window frames. You name it we painted it.

That summer I flew out with my brother Tony to see Mum who had moved to Spain the previous summer. Two weeks in Malaga was just the ticket and a break from all that painting. Tanned and refreshed, it was back to pre-season. Greenwich Park, Peak Freans. Oh the glamorous life of a professional footballer!

I was still on £7 per week. After a slow start to the season Smethy finally got a run in the side. This was the season that ex-Tottenham and Southampton star Frank Saul signed for the club. He came in on the last day of the March transfer deadline. I grew up as a fanatical Spurs supporter. I knew that as a young man Frank had been part of the 60/61 double-winning squad which included players like Dave Mackay, Danny Blanchflower and Bobby Smith, who Bobby Pittaway and I had played against in that recent Midweek League reserve game.

The first day that 'Sauly' turned up for training I was a bit starry-eyed. Frank, like Derek Smethurst, didn't get into the side straightaway Ned and I gravitated towards Frank. He was a very warm and friendly guy and was very happy to have us in his company. It wasn't long before, driving home after training, all three of us would visit the Crown and Anchor pub for a lager and the best salmon doorstep sandwich in the area! We both came to idolise Frank. He was a blunt, down-to-earth, grounded individual and didn't suffer fools easily. You could see in training that he had been a good player, perhaps the legs were no longer there, but he was such a good technician that legs didn't matter.

He made his debut in a thrilling 3-3 away draw at Carlisle. I had been chosen to travel and was thrilled when Frank asked me to room with him. Before we got ready to sleep, I finally got to ask him about that Spurs double-winning side. He was only 17 when he was in that squad and went on to play 118 games for Spurs. Only four years previous he had scored the winning goal in the 1967 cup final against London rivals Chelsea.

I freely admit I was in awe of him. He taught me so many things including how to drink and pull a member of the opposite sex. I had just turned 16 and hung on his every word. Every day when our jobs were done, Ned and I would take a ball onto the pitch and ping it to one another. This was so enjoyable, until Roy the groundsman caught us and shouted "Get off my fucking pitch!"

These ball sessions between the two of us were more productive than almost all of those useless training sessions we had to endure at Deptford Park. Luckily for Ned and I, we would work a lot with Billy Neil. Which at least gave us an end product something educational where our football development was concerned.

Once pre-season before the start of 72/73 finished I had three weeks until my 18th birthday and the big decision as to whether I would be offered a professional contract. I couldn't get out of my head the sight of John Flaherty coming down the stairs from the secretary's office only a few months previously absolutely devastated because he had been turned down.

He was sobbing his heart out and couldn't be consoled. Ned and I were also devastated as John was a big pal. We both felt that John signing pro was a no brainer. Sadly John was left to find his way in the big wide world alone. Football was cruel in those days and not making it left huge mental scars and the reality of not being in the game was so damaging.

That pre-season saw the first team play three friendlies at home to Scottish teams like Forfar Ayr United. Ned and I secretly hoped we might be involved. The first Saturday of the season saw the first team beat Hull city 2-0 with Smethy starting and scoring along with Gordon Bolland. It was now only four days from my birthday so for the next few days I was wracked with doubt about my future.

Ned would tell me encouragingly: "Don't worry, you're too good to be turned down.". Then, on the following Wednesday, I was summoned to the managers office to hear my fate.

John Flaherty - Started on the same day as each other, big friend. Confirmed apprentice contract March 1967

Benny Fenton - First team manager

Jack Blackman - First Team Physiotherapist and father figure

Pat Lally - Tough centre half but a great bloke

FROM THE DEN TO WEMBLEY

Keith Weller - First Team star player , highly talented

.Derek Smethurst - New summer signing.

Derek Possee and author - Derek and I sat together on my first day as an apprentice

George Duck

Andy Nelson - First Team Coach

Team Photo with all apprentices

4
TURNING PRO

I climbed the stairs very tentatively and, when at the top, club secretary Mr Borland opened the door for me and shook my hand, saying: "Good luck Tom".

I turned half left to knock on the Gaffer's door/ I heard from inside: "Come in Thomas". I entered and looking at the floor, mumbled "Hello Boss".

The last time I had been in this situation my Mum was with me to sign my apprentice contract three years ago. He gestured me to sit down as well as asking the secretary to take a chair as well.

He then reached down to a drawer in his large opulent desk.

He pulled out an A4 blue coloured document as he had done three years ago. He opened it and, placing it in front of me said: "Thomas, I have great pleasure in offering you your first professional contract."

He then said: "This contract is for one year. You will receive a basic salary of £40.00 per week.' He then turned to the secretary and said "Gordon, Thomas will be part of the official first team squad and shall be paid all of the relevant bonuses".

He then asked the secretary to witness my contract with his signature. I then signed my contract. The Gaffer then congratulated me saying what a great attitude I had and this contract was a reward for all my hard work in the last three years.

On leaving Benny's office I asked Mr Borland what did all relevant bonuses mean. He replied: "Tom, when you open your contract you will see a list of bonuses that, as a first team squad member, you are entitled to."

I put the contract under my tracksuit top so later on I could read it in private. On leaving the secretary's office I looked down the stairs to see Ned, Smethy and Frank waiting for me. I walked down the stairs and yelped "YES!" They all walked up towards me offering their hands. Once I accepted their congratulations I made my way to the home team dressing room to see Jack. He gave me warm handshake and a proper bear hug.

"I shall miss working with you Tom. You deserve this, You are a credit to yourself" he said. Those words meant the world to me. Jack had watched me play every one of those Midweek League reserve team games. Praise from him was high praise indeed. He then said: "Get yourself a shower and get off home, you're a pro now".

I dried myself off and Frank, Ned me and Smethy drove to the Crown and Anchor for a celebratory drink and sandwich.

I still had to get on that number 21 bus home again and the contract was still under my tracksuit top. I felt really pleased and thought to myself that when I got home I will ring Mum out in Spain and tell her the good news. I phoned Gordon Bolland as well, he was also delighted for me and told me he would pick me up in the morning and give me a lift into training.

The club was still reeling from missing promotion to Division One the previous season, Norwich, Birmingham and ourselves were in a three-way tussle for an automatic promotion spot all season. Norwich won the league eventually but who can ever forget that last home game of the season when Possee and Bridges scored a goal apiece to secure a 2 -0 win over Preston North End. Leaving us one point in front of our bitter rivals Birmingham City for automatic promotion.

Birmingham's last match was away at Leyton Orient the following Tuesday evening. A win would see them take second place and pip us to promotion. A couple of the players - Eamon Dunphy and Alan Dorney - went over to watch. It must have been difficult as Birmingham won 1-0 ending our chances to play Division One football.

When I got home that night having not long signed pro, the thought of what might have been entered my head. If the club had been promoted its not beyond the bounds of possibility that, having signed pro, I could have made my debut away to Manchester United at Old Trafford. Who knows?

Opening my contract that night I read through the bonuses I would be eligible for. I would receive £25.00 for every point we won. From being an £8 per week apprentice this felt like I was a real professional footballer. Also there was a few pounds for place money. My girlfriend was really excited. It meant we could see more of each other and perhaps save some money towards getting our own place. The next big challenge for me was passing my driving test in three weeks' time.

FROM THE DEN TO WEMBLEY

Gordon Bolland - My lift!

Peter Taylor - Dumped me on my backside!

Graham Souness - "Jock!" "Too good for me!"

Steve Brown - Signing Pro - Sarcastic!

Jim Standen - Goalkeeper, great professional, learnt so much from him

Jack Burkett, full-back, man of real quality, immaculate in everything he did, great role model

5
DROPPING DOWN

The guy teaching me to drive was an ex-copper called Bill Emerson. He had taught my Mum a few years ago. He finally told me I was ready for my test, so on that day in early September 1972, I drove Bill's dual controlled Ford Escort to the test centre at Hither Green Lane near Lewisham. Getting out of the car, Bill shook my hand and wished me luck. I don't know if I have ever felt so nervous (even walking up those stairs to Benny's' office to learn if I was going to get that professional contract).

About 30 minutes after leaving the test centre I pulled up back to where I had started. After a couple of highway code questions the examiner turned towards me and said "Congratulation, Mr Sampson you have passed your test."

I got out and Bill gave me the thumbs up. I smiled at him and returned his gesture. Bill let me drive home where Tony was waiting for me. He congratulated me and after handing me the keys to Mum's old Ford Anglia, I got in behind the wheel and with my new found professional footballer wealth drove to the petrol station and filled my new car up with fuel which cost about five pounds eighty five pence!

With the season only three weeks old I was named on the bench away to Cardiff days after passing my driving test. Sadly the game ended in a 0-1 defeat.

Alf Wood, a £45.000 buy from Shrewsbury, was now leading the line. His signing came as a result of Barry Bridges moving to Brighton for £29.000 the previous

May. I was really sorry to see Barry go but Alf was a very approachable guy and friendly. I never really got to know him very well but he was happy to give his time, and again, with my professional football career still in its infancy, he was only too happy to offer words of wisdom. After the Cardiff trip it was back to the Midweek League reserve team. I have to admit that I felt more confident now that I had signed pro. I felt I had to be more responsible for the team. I would get on the ball for free kicks and take responsibility for what type of delivery was required. Little details were important to me. I felt I had to be more vocal in the dressing room before the game.

This was the season that I became great friends with Billy Neil. Billy had signed for previous manager Billy Gray and was part of that side that boasted that long unbeaten home run in the mid-sixties. That was probably the first Millwall side I ever saw. Lawrie Leslie in goal, John Gilchrist at right-back, Harry Cripps or Pat Brady left-back. Tommy Wilson and Brian Snowdon central defenders, Joey Broadfoot right wing, Billy left wing, Harry Obeney midfield with Barry Rowan, Len Julians at centre Forward.

Now I was a full pro, Billy took it upon himself to guide me in the right direction. Billy was eight years older than me. We lived round the corner from each other so often gave each other lifts when required. I genuinely loved the man. With my new found wealth, I bought a set of second-hand golf clubs because now I was driving to training, Smethy and I could go and play golf in the afternoons. I had played a lot of weekend golf with my brother Tony so I quite fancied myself.

After training Derek and I would follow each other in the direction of Croydon where we played most of our golf. We became very close friends. Derek was driving a very up-market Lancia Fulvia whilst I was trotting around in my Mum's old two tone Ford Anglia. Whenever we arrived at the golf club we had booked to play, Smethy playfully told me not to park next to him! "Fucking snob!" I used to tell him. He was a 'lefty' and, like his football, very stylish.

I was your regular right-hander and an ordinary 18 handicapper. If Benny had found out Derek and I were on the golf course four days per week he would have done his nut. He didn't like his players playing golf in midweek. He believed it affected your legs in a negative way. Smethy wasn't bothered because he couldn't command a regular place in the first team, much to his disgust.

They weren't pulling up any trees at all, hovering around mid-table which was disappointing because everybody had been so optimistic at the start.

In early March we were due to play away at Leyton Orient who were fighting for their lives in the lower reaches of the table. For this game central defender Barry Kitchener was suspended so there was much conjecture as to what the Gaffer would do. I wondered if I might find myself playing alongside Alan Dorney in central defence with Dennis behind sweeping up.

In anticipation, I did a bit of homework on our next opponents. I found out that ex-Nottingham Forest European Cup winner Ian Bowyer had been playing in the number nine shirt in recent games, so I thought height wouldn't be a problem, nor will pace. Admittedly he was a vastly experienced player, but I was so confident at that time the only question was if Benny Fenton would have the same confidence in this young charge of his.

On the Friday before the game, the 9th of March 1973, I was named as a substitute but Smethy was in at number nine. It looked like Alf Wood would be playing central defender alongside Alan Dorney with Derek playing up front instead of Alf. The following day we all met up at 2pm in the away dressing room.

I had played many times at Brisbane Road in reserve and youth team games but only in front of a handful of people. I got changed almost next to Smethy.

Benny gave his team talk and warned the guys that Orient were fighting for their Division Two lives, so to expect a really tough game. Also absent today was the injured Derek Possee, so Smethy would have to be supported by wide men Dougie Allder (left) and Steve Brown (right) with Alf Wood marking ex-Crystal Palace man Gerry Queen with Alan doing a job on Bowyer.

On a pleasant early March afternoon the game kicked off on a very dry and bumpy pitch. Eamon and Gordon were struggling to get their foot on the ball because of the uneven surface. Browny and Dougie were starved of the ball and Smethy was getting little change out of Orient's big physical centre half Paul Harris. I knew Paul from our reserve team battles. The Gaffer was going ballistic on the bench as we were getting pushed around far too easily. Then he put his arm on mine just before half time and whispered: "Thomas I should have played you and kept Alf up front. Alan could have dealt with Queen and you could have handled the little ginger shit Bowyer!" I acknowledged him quietly.

We went in at half time 0-1 down. Benny launched into one, berating players for their lack of heart. I sat back quietly and thought that wasn't fair. The pitch was beating both teams. Gordon Bolland equalised 15 minutes into the second half from the spot. At the restart, Benny nudged me and said: "Go and get warmed up son."

So I got up, jogged up and down the touchline and did some stretches. Benny then called me back to the bench and said: "Get stripped, you're going on. I'm bringing Derek off and pushing Alf back up front."

"Tell Alan to deal with Queen and you do a job on Bowyer."

My heart was pounding as I ran onto the pitch. Orient won a free kick way out wide and as we all lined up waiting for the kick to come in, I attached myself to the "ginger shit" like I did to Ronnie Howell that day at Deptford Park when I was 13. Alan was marking Queen. Just before the kick was delivered Bowyer clipped my nose with his left elbow and I went down clutching my face. I heard the whistle go, I jumped up to see England's premier referee Jack Taylor admonishing Bowyer.

Taylor would go on to referee next year's World Cup final between West Germany and Holland. Luckily the free kick came to nothing. Jogging back up to the halfway line, Taylor pulled me aside and said: "Son, if you want to get your own back, don't let me see it!" Fair play I thought.

With 20 minutes to go we were still in it. I spent that last quarter of the match trying to take retribution out on Bowyer. While trying to push on and get both points, Orient stunned us with two late goals to give the scoreline a lopsided look. I was really pleased with my contribution despite the loss. I had now made my Football League bow - albeit only 35 minutes. I phoned Ned when I got home to tell him I was now a genuine first team player. He naturally was delighted for me. He had signed pro last October and after all those years together I had won the race to break into the first team. He was a beast of a midfielder. Tall, great balance and a complete range of passing. I knew it wouldn't be long before his turn would come. Sure enough a month later there was Mick's name at number ten replacing Eamon Dunphy in central midfield at home to Sheffield Wednesday. I watched Ned from the back of the stand that day, proud like a big brother watching his younger sibling shining in the spotlight.

The week after making my debut the first team were at home to Preston North End. I knew I had no chance of playing as Barry Kitchener was now available again but I was hoping that at least I would get a place on the bench. The guys swept lowly Preston aside 4-1 with two goals from Gordon Bolland and one each from Harry and Alf. I had loads of people come up to me and congratulate me for how well I had played last week after coming on as a sub.

I watched the Preston game with all of the apprentices in front of the groundsman's shed near the end of the players tunnel. I was hoping that I would at least get a crack at starting in the side before the season finished. I also imagined Ned and I starting in the same game together. There were only nine games left and we were in mid-table with nothing left to play for, an ideal time for me to get a game but sadly I was left out in the cold for those last matches.

After watching Mick make his debut against Sheffield Wednesday he then started four of the next five games. I thought to myself I would not show how disappointed I was by treating those last few Midweek League reserve games as first team matches.

With the close season almost upon us I wanted to impress Benny and hopefully give him something to think about during the break. Smethy and I hit the golf courses that summer, playing a couple of dozen or so rounds. In that break he was considering his options because of not establishing himself after three seasons in the club. He finished the 72/73 season with a few starts and a couple of goals. Young trialist Gordon Hill was now in the club so along with Ned and young David Coxhill 'Smethy' knew he was facing more competition for next season.

One of his options was on the other side of the Atlantic where football was gradually getting a foothold in the American people's imagination. Derek was weighing up an offer from Tampa Bay Rowdies. I would miss him if he did decide to go because we had become very close friends. Derek did eventually decide to go stateside where he enjoyed a very successful career with the Rowdies.

My bubble was well and truly burst during that close season when I read in the local paper that Benny had signed two young full backs. Eddie Jones a young left-back from Tottenham as well as 19-year-old right-back Dave Donaldson from Arsenal. This meant I had fallen even further down the pecking order. I knew both Eddie and Dave from our youth team days. One of the few places I felt I could force my way into the first team was at full-back, left or right.

This double signing left me feeling really down-hearted as I now realised that Midweek League reserve football was going to be my only source of game time for the foreseeable future. I spoke with several people before we returned for the 73/74 season. Frank, Billy and Gordon all told me to get my head down in pre-season and play as well as I can every time I played. Then, when the season was well underway, to go and see the Gaffer and ask him about possibly going out on loan somewhere. I did ring Andy Nelson at Gillingham to see if he would take me on loan or perhaps full time. George Jacks and David Coxhill had already followed Andy to The Gills so if it happened I would have friends in the club. Andy told me he had a very tight budget so it would have to be a loan and not full time.

Three weeks into the new season I went to see Benny to see if I could go out on loan somewhere he said he would circulate my name to all the teams in the south east region. Very soon after this Dave and Eddie replaced Harry Cripps and Brian Brown at right and left back. About this time Ned got a run of five games on the bounce. Two days later Andy Nelson rang me to say he had received a circular from Millwall to say that I was available for a transfer but any club wanting to take me would have to pay £5000. I was crushed because here I was, 19 years of age with 35 minutes of first team football behind me. Who would pay that much for someone so inexperienced?

I went to see the Gaffer, pretending I didn't know about this fee business. He then told me that Harry Gregg the ex-Manchester United goalkeeping legend and now manager of Swansea wanted to take me on loan. I looked at Benny and said I'd heard from Andy Nelson that you were asking a fee for me. He replied: "Yes. £5000".

I plucked up some courage and said: "That's ridiculous" and in the same breath I said: "I ain't going to Swansea on loan either. Where would I stay?"

He said to me that Swansea would cover the cost of my digs. I thought about it for a millisecond and replied: "No way".

When I told Frank and Billy about the fee they advised me that I could take the club to a tribunal and fight it. I contacted the Football Association and asked their advice. They asked for my side of the story and said they would write to the club asking that they state their reasons for asking for a fee. I would then have to wait until the club responded. I felt a bit self-conscious for the next couple of weeks because it was a big thing for me challenging the club this way.

The season didn't start well for the first team taking only one point from six games and there followed the usual Monday morning inquests. I was still having to do my best in those meaningless reserve games. I was determined to shrug off my predicament. I received a letter from the FA telling me that they had informed the club that the £5000 fee was not in-keeping with my experience and therefore I should be granted a free transfer.

FROM THE DEN TO WEMBLEY

I was obviously delighted with this decision and rang Andy Nelson to tell him and ask if he would be interested in signing me. He told me he had a surplus of players in his squad at the present time and said he would have to think about it for a couple of days.

I was disappointed because foolishly I had let myself believe there was a new start for me.

I suddenly started to enjoy myself playing reserve team football because it was mostly made up of all my old apprentice mates. Bobby Pittaway and I were starting to form a kind of telepathic relationship in the centre of that reserve team defensive partnership. Bob was looking to sign his first professional contract in a few months time so playing well in the reserves wasn't doing him any harm.

Robin Wainwright had then joined the club on a free transfer from Luton. His situation there mirrored mine. So breaking free for him gave me a little bit more optimism. Robin and I became good friends. He was a languid stylish midfield player. Benny was coming under more and more pressure as results were going from bad to worse. Ned was getting increasingly frustrated at the lack of game time. Gordon Hill had forced his way into the first team on the left wing and he was starting to make a real name for himself with some breathtaking goals and flashes of genius. All of the top clubs were starting to take notice of him and rumours of him leaving for a big fee and a big club covered the back pages.

We were coming to the end of the 73/74 season. It was over a year since I'd made my debut. Jones and Donaldson had become first team regulars ousting Harry Cripps and Brian Brown. I was increasingly frustrated with the way my career was going. I phoned Charlton's youth team manager Les Gore who had followed my career since I was 12 years of age. I asked him to ask

Charlton first team manager Theo Foley if he would be interested in signing me for the following season.

Les came back to me a couple of days later saying Theo would definitely take me but it had to be a free transfer. I assured Les that was fine. Waiting for the season to finish felt like an eternity and during the equally frustrating close season my girlfriend and I spent a couple of weeks on the Isle of Wight.

When pre-season started I played in all of the friendlies against non-league sides. Benny had kindly extended my contract by one year. He didn't have to do it. I hoped he was rewarding me for all that hard work I had put in for the past three years.

I was shocked when just after the turn of the year I heard that Charlton had sacked Foley. He had signed Eamon Dunphy and Harry Cripps from us just weeks before. I thought it was a strange decision. The day after, I found out I was playing for the Midweek League side at home to Watford and I spied Theo watching the game from halfway up the Cold Blow Lane terrace.

When the game finished Benny called me upstairs to see him in his office when I got there he told me Dartford of the Southern League wanted to take me on loan for a month. Dartford were the current league champions and only a few months ago had appeared in the FA Trophy Final at Wembley losing narrowly to Morecambe 1-2.

The Darts had sacked legendary manager and former Gillingham striker Ernie Morgan. They had approached Theo to be interim manager until they could appoint someone else. That then explained why Theo was watching the Watford game. Theo phoned me at home that evening to tell me I needed to sign the relevant forms so could I go to his house tomorrow morning. Theo lived just off of Shooters Hill near Blackheath, so I said yeah fine no problem. He then told me my debut would be tomorrow evening away to arch rivals

Maidstone United. He also told me Millwall would continue to pay my wages, and for every game I played for Dartford whilst on loan I would receive an extra £30 appearance money, so for the next four weeks I would be quids in.

Theo told me to meet the coach at Dartford's Watling Street ground for 5:30 the following evening. When I arrived I got out of my car carrying my boots and shin pads in the Dartford kit bag Theo had given me. I looked up and saw a familiar face in Micky Shovelar. Mick was an ex-Arsenal youth team player and we knew each other very well. Sitting alongside each other I picked Mick's brain as to what to expect.

Theo arrived and on seeing me he got me up and proceeded to introduce me to everyone. I noticed that everybody looked a lot older than me. Sitting back down with Mick he was giggling and said: "How many names can you remember?" "None" I replied. He then went on to tell me: "We've been struggling this season. It's important we get something tonight".

"What sort of crowd will there be?" I enquired.

"About 2000", he answered. I raised my eyebrows and thought: that's a few more than the 20-odd watching yesterdays reserve team game against Watford!

As we set off Theo wanted me to meet my central defensive partner for the game. He sat me down next to this thick-set slightly balding guy and said: "Tom, meet a great friend of mine: Graham Carr." I shook hands with Graham and he said to me in a broad Geordie accent: "Hello son".

Graham looked like he could handle himself. I was to find out in my month's loan that would be a huge understatement. Arriving at Maidstone's ground, I followed everyone into the away dressing room. It was painted in a sort of bright yellow and had a decent size medical room I really didn't know what to expect, but having played against non-league sides in numerous pre-season friendlies this was definitely a step up.

Kit man Lennie Prescott - a lifelong Dartford fan - was handing out shirts, shorts and socks. This was the first difference I noticed, because playing professionally all the kit was laid out before you arrived.

While we were getting changed Theo pinned up the teamsheet and after that he started to tell us all what he expected of us. This was not only an important game because of our league position it also carried with it bragging rights for both sets of supporters.

During the warm up I tried to familiarise myself with everyone. The average age of our team I guessed at about 32-35. Here I was just turned 19 and not a clue what to expect. The game kicked off in the pouring rain. I settled in alongside Graham. The atmosphere was raucous, this was a world away from Midweek League football. Maidstone were obviously a good side, knocking it around on a very slick pitch. With 25 minutes gone in the first half we were awarded a penalty for a handball. The Maidstone players surrounded the referee to protest. When it all calmed down Theo was shouting for me to step up and take it. I hadn't taken a penalty since I was at school.

Walking forward I was thinking hit it as hard as you can. When I reached the penalty spot it was sat in a tiny recess and full of water. I tried to kick it dry and at least flatten it. When I finally placed the ball on the spot I wasn't very happy with it and the run up to the ball was very muddy. Eventually I turned around to face Maidstone 'keeper Derek Bellotti. I jogged to the ball and as I struck it my standing foot gave way and it rose up quickly and clipped the crossbar.

I was distraught.

My new colleagues did their best to console me. The game re-started and I tried to put the penalty miss behind me. Just before half time Maidstone took the lead and we trudged in at half time a goal down. I was apologising to everyone for missing the penalty. Everybody was very encouraging. I had actually played very well and Graham and I had found a good understanding. He had won every aerial battle, I just dropped off and cleared up anything that dropped.

I was physically as strong as I'd ever been and my level of fitness was excellent. I made up for my penalty miss when, five minutes into the second half, I stepped into midfield, intercepting a wayward Maidstone pass. I travelled 20 yards and struck a shot which for the second time in the match hit the crossbar rebounding to ace Dartford striker Tommy Henderson who tapped home. Everyone ran to me like I had just scored the equaliser. Waiting for Maidstone to kick off, Graham shook my hand and said: "Well done son."

The game finished all square and we had won an invaluable point. The attendance was officially 2749. Despite the penalty miss I had not enjoyed myself so much for ages. In the dressing room after the game Theo congratulated me on my performance. On the coach going back to Dartford, Micky Shovelar and I chatted about the game and what a great point we had won. I told him how much I had enjoyed my first game. He very kindly said: "Tom you were outstanding" I thought to myself what a great month this was going to be.

I was still training with Millwall so the following morning I was in early to tell of the events of the night before. I felt great and not tired from the match. I was thinking about all of the part-time guys that I had played with last night. They would all be at work now doing their nine to five ritual and here I was out in the fresh air training. The only player in the dressing room that understood the non-league world was goalkeeper Bryan King who started at Southern league side Chelmsford City.

On the day of my Dartford debut Steve Brown signed for Maidstone whilst Bobby Pittaway went to Kingy's old team Chelmsford. All three of us were embarking on new adventures. Bob had signed a professional contract in recent months but knew his chances of getting a first-team spot were slim with Barry Kitchener a fixture in the side. So moving to Chelmsford was a positive move and not a backward step. As for Browny, he had become a permanent sub.

After training I got home and Theo rang me to tell me The Darts' next game was this coming Saturday away to Yeovil. He then told me I wouldn't be needed. Before I could protest, he told me the player I had replaced against Maidstone was club legend and captain Les Burns. Les's career was drawing to a close and Theo wanted to give him one more game which obviously I understood.

The following Saturday I went to watch the first team play Luton. Smethy was starting and scored in a thrilling 3-2 win with Gordon Bolland getting a brace.

In the bar upstairs after the game Derek told me he would be leaving the club this June to go and play for Tampa Bay Rowdies. I told him how sorry I would be to see him go,but there was enough time left to get a few rounds of golf in.

Later that evening I rang Mick shovelar to hear that Dartford had lost 2-4 at Yeovil.

Our next game was the following Tuesday at home to Romford. Theo phoned me on Sunday afternoon to confirm I would be starting. I was really looking forward to playing at home for the first time.

My home debut went really well, beating our fellow strugglers 3-0. That result helped Dartford move out of the bottom three. I couldn't understand how they could have found themselves in this precarious position. I had played two games for them and it seemed to me that we were a good side. Mick Shovelar explained to me that injuries and suspensions had cost them dearly at the start of the season. I had played two games and had felt really at home, I just couldn't imagine going back to aimless reserve team football when my loan was over.

The two games I played attracted over 3000 people. It was March 1974 and I returned to Millwall. Things weren't looking too rosy for the first team, their results saw them languishing in the lower half of the table. Two weeks after returning to the club, Benny Fenton was sacked and Lawrie Leslie was put in charge.

I have always said Lawrie was a lovely man. Unfortunately, managing the first team was a little bit above his pay grade. The only good thing about Lawrie being in charge was that I had a decent chance of getting a game. Lawrie did in fact take me to Norwich as a sub. They had won Division Two when Birmingham pipped us to a place in Division One a couple of seasons ago, but they had come back down. I had the pleasure that day of watching probably the best front two of that era in Ted McDougall and Phil Boyer.

That weekend Theo rang to tell me that ex-Queens Park Rangers manager Gordon Jago was to be announced as The Lions' new manager on Monday.

He went on to tell me he was joining Jago as first team coach. I went into training on Monday with a spring in my step. Working under Theo again was going to be brilliant. There was a flurry of activity outside the car park with both journalists and photographers waiting to hear the news. The Chairman's car was also there.

The upstairs tearoom had been set up to hold a press conference. While I was parking my car, Theo drove in with Jago in his. I nodded to Theo and followed the pair of them into the dressing room where most of the players were changed into their matchday kit.

Theo and Jago then disappeared upstairs to be officially unveiled. Ten minutes later chairman Micky Purser walked into the dressing room with Gordon and Theo to officially introduce the pair. When Purser left, Gordon addressed the players.

He assured them that things were going to change for the better. Training would be more instructive and productive. I was brimming with excitement. Jago was known for his expansive style of football. He then said we would be training at Crystal Palace the following day on the grass pitch behind the main stand.

That session made a great impression on me. It was clever but not too complicated, every one was smiling and enjoying it. The session was all ball-orientated. The days of Deptford Park and two seven-a-side games were long forgotten.

Theo imposed his personality all over the session, cajoling and joking with players. What a pleasure it was going to be to come to "work" over the next few weeks.

Theo would have some of the young players back in the afternoon mainly practising shooting, crossing and movement. Me, Ned, George Duck, Roy Compton, Malcolm Hobbs, Kenny Enver, Malcolm Davies and Billy Holmes gained so much from those afternoon sessions.

It was after one of them that Theo told me that the Gaffer wanted to see me in his office.

Jago had been in the club about three weeks and had seen me play three reserve team games. I knocked on his door and entered nervously.

Jago got up from his desk and shook my hand. He said: "Tom, Theo has told me you are a very good player, it is my intention to build my team around some of the younger players like you".

The he got up and said: "I have got someone I would like you to meet."

I asked him: "Am I still on the transfer list?"

"That's up to you son" he replied.

I followed him into the tearoom where a middle-aged man was sitting in the corner pouring himself a cup of tea. Gordon said: "Vic, this is Tommy Sampson".

Vic and I shook hands, Gordon then turned to me and said "Tom this is a good friend of mine Vic Crowe. He wants to talk with you and make you a proposition." He then carried on by saying Vic played many years for Aston Villa as well as England.

I sat down at the table whilst Vic poured me a cup of tea. He looked at me and said: "Tom, I suppose you are wondering what this is all about?"

"I have just taken over as the manager of Portland Timbers in the new North American Soccer League and I would like you to consider joining us" he continued.

The club would pay my air fare and put me in suitable accommodation when I got there'. I knew the American Soccer League was growing and I hesitantly said: "Can I think about it for a couple of days?"

He replied: "Yes sure I didn't expect an answer today!"

He gave me his card and told me to give him a call when I was ready. Before I could get up to leave he said: "Oh by the way, I've just signed my first player. Clyde Best from West Ham."

"OK" I said, turning to leave, "I will call you soon" and drove home in a daze.

That night I got a phone call from legendary Charlton defender Peter Reeves. One of the last things Theo did before leaving Dartford was to sign Peter. When Theo finally left to go to Millwall as first team coach the Dartford board appointed Peter as player- manager. Sadly after both Theo and I left, Dartford were relegated from the Southern Premier League to the Southern League Division One South. Peter's remit was to win promotion back to the Southern Premier League at the first time of asking. He had rung to ask me to consider signing for The Darts again.

I had made a great impression during my month's loan at Watling Street and I had lots of things to consider. I spoke to Billy Neil to ask his advice. He was as perplexed as me as to what to do. My only doubt about Portland Timbers was that the football scene in the States was in its infancy and in England it was viewed with a great deal of scepticism.

I rang Peter Reeves back to find out what was on offer. He said it was a one year contract. I would be paid £40 per week and £10 appearance money and because I was coming on a free transfer, the club will give me a £1,000 signing on fee when I signed my contract.

I wrestled with my conscience for a week before I decided to sign for Dartford. I phoned Mr Crowe to tell him I was staying in England, he was very gracious and wished me well. I phoned Theo to tell him of my decision and he told me to leave it with him and that he'd tell the secretary in the morning.

I told Peter Reeves that the Dartford secretary should make contact with his Millwall counterpart so that all the relevant paperwork could be done. I phoned Ned to tell him what I had decided to do. He was a bit sceptical at first, saying: "Are you sure you want to drop out of the league?

"No, I'm not!" I replied.

But since Jago had been Millwall manager I had been nowhere near a first team place. So much for building a side around young players like me! His first couple of signings were Tony Hazell from QPR and full back Ray Evans from Tottenham. Looking back all these years later I regret not going to America, but hindsight is a gift nobody is blessed with. That first season at Dartford we won promotion back to the Southern Premier League.

I captained the side that season and was voted Supporters' Player of the Year. It was such an exciting season, constantly looking at the league table and I remember it with such fondness but Peter's reward for winning promotion was the sack!

It was believed that the Dartford Board felt he wouldn't be experienced enough to step up into The Southern League Premier. So the club had all of the close season to find another manager, a scenario that was very unsettling.

Luckily for me, the club had taken up the option on my contract to stay another year. I had agreed with Peter that I would receive £30 per week during the close season. I rang the secretary to ask him how I was going to get paid. He said ring me back tomorrow because he would have to talk to the chairman. I rang the Dartford secretary back the following day and he told me if I came to his house on a Friday evening, I would get my money in cash.

As the summer moved on there were numerous rumours about the new manager. Countless names were thrown around until finally, on the cusp of pre-season training starting, the announcement came my new manager would be ex-Tooting and Mitcham boss Roy Dwight.

Dwight had steered Tooting to a wonderful FA Cup run the season before, beating Football League side Swindon Town after a replay. Roy also played for Nottingham Forest, famously breaking his leg in the 1959 FA Cup final against Luton Town which Forest won 2-1. He also was Elton John's cousin.

Roy's number two was to be ex-Dartford player and legend John Stevens. With Elton John being Watford

Chairman, it was no surprise when, during pre-season, a number of players with a Watford connection joined the club.

Pat Morrissey, Brian Greenhalgh, Vic Akers, Ronnie Walton all were established players. The new season started badly with a first day 1-4 home defeat to league favourites Nuneaton Town, followed by a battling 1-1 home draw with Kettering Town who were led by ex Wolves legend player-manager Derek Dougan. Roy also enlisted Graham Dennis from Isthmian Leaguers Carshalton Athletic. The Isthmian League was a 'gentleman's league' in contrast to the 'ruffian' Southern League and poor Graham struggled to come to terms with it.

I befriended Graham to try and help him find his form but that season was a struggle. Roy's style of management was very low-key and a bit bland. Before that season finished Ned had joined along with ex-Millwall colleague Alan Dorney. One of Roy's big stellar signings was Arthur Horsfield, a loan signing from Watford. Also arriving was central defender Ben Embery (ex-Spurs and Exeter City) from Gravesend and Northfleet.

Roy and I had a fractious relationship. He obviously didn't rate me and by the time I left Dartford in 1989/90 he had been replaced by former player Graham Carr. Roy lost his job in very controversial circumstances.

We had been drawn away to Leatherhead in the fourth qualifying round of the FA Cup. The rain had been torrential all week, on the way people were questioning if the game would be on or not. The coach parked up on the Elmers End roundabout. Roy's assistant Johnny Stevens was sent to a public telephone box to see if the game was still on. John called Leatherhead FC explaining that we were Dartford FC and was the game still on. By now it was 1:45pm. The answer came back that the game was off. John got back on the coach and told Roy. The coach returned to where the players had been picked up and left their cars.

Getting back in our cars we all headed back home and while I was watching Match of the Day that evening, Jimmy Hill read out a piece that Dartford had not turned up at Leatherhead for the very important fourth qualifying round tie!

I immediately rang John Stevens to ask what had gone on. He said: "Yes, we never turned up, I was given the wrong information!".

He then told me the game had been rescheduled for the following Tuesday and the coach would pick players up at Elmers End at 6 o'clock. During that three day interval the country endured heavy snowfall and the south east was heavily hit. Jumping on the coach that Tuesday night John Stevens received tremendous stick about the incident the previous Saturday. Getting to Leatherhead the pitch was covered in three inches of snow. The game was delayed by at least fifteen minutes to allow Leatherhead's amateur international goalkeeper John Swannel to arrive at the ground.

We kicked off using a white football, but after just ten minutes it was swapped for an orange one. John Swannel turned up at 7:45pm and we were already 0-2 down, going on to lose 2-5.

Within two days of this debacle Roy was out of a job with Stevens taking over temporarily. I wasn't sorry to see Roy go. I had five great seasons at Dartford, playing 221 games and I left with a very heavy heart. I was just 27 years of age and considered over the hill!

FROM THE DEN TO WEMBLEY

Branded as a tout— and he's just 16!

By PATRICK COLLINS

A 16-YEAR-OLD apprentice who sold his only Cup Final ticket is one of the victims of the Football Association's war on touts.

The boy, who has made reserve team appearances for Second Division Millwall, allowed his ticket for the Wembley terraces to fall into the hands of the spivs.

Banned

The ticket was traced, an investigation began during the summer, and the boy's punishment is a place among the 11 players who have been banned from receiving tickets for the next five years.

The FA have decided not to name any of the 11—not of whom are bigger figures than a Millwall apprentice.

But in a week when Jeff Astle could boast of making £200 from the sale of Cup tickets, it will seem to many people that the FA would have been better employed in catching the big fish rather than jumping upon erring apprentices.

Certainly it seems that way to Professional Footballers' Association chairman Derek Dougan who is angry both with the FA and Astle.

"The speculation of the past few days has been appalling," Dougan told me.

"All I've heard for days is: 'Is he one of the 11, is he of it, or could it be him?' And this sort of thing is bound to happen when the FA can't find the moral courage to reveal the names.

"Astle's outburst has been no help at all. If he's given the public the impression that players up and down the country are making hundreds of pounds by selling tickets, then he's way off target.

Simple

"I represent nearly 3,000 players. I know that only a tiny percentage of these make money out of selling tickets.

"The FA know this, too. If they care to sit down with us and talk about it, we might solve the problem.

"But it won't be solved by clobbering apprentices."

And what, in Dougan's view, is the solution? "It couldn't be more simple: 'Print the names of the players on the tickets. Everyone would then know where they came from. It's obvious."

Tommy the tout - Headline - News of the World

Laurie Leslie - New first team coach 71-72 - nice guy but limited

Barry Bridges - ex England International, the ultimate pro's pro

Me and Bobby Pittaway - telepathic understanding

FROM THE DEN TO WEMBLEY

The legendary Harry Cripps

Barry Kitchener - the best centre half outside of Division One

Dennis Burnett (above on left of Alf Wood and Harry Cripps) - sweeper, I admired Dennis as a player.

Kenny Enver (right) - kind-hearted soul and talented footballer

FROM THE DEN TO WEMBLEY

Derek Smethurst and car

Frank Saul

Gordon Jago

Peter Reeves

Graham Carr

FROM THE DEN TO WEMBLEY

The Den, home of Millwall FC

Theo Foley, huge influence on my career, a great man to play for

Billy Neil - Great friend and mentor

6
MOVING ON

When people heard that I had been released by Dartford my phone didn't stop ringing. One of those calls was from Welling United's manager Graham Hobbins. Welling were an Athenian League side. I was now living in Peckham with my girlfriend in a lovely two bedroom apartment. Graham invited me to Welling's first game of the season. They had started as a junior Sunday League side, who I nearly signed for when I was eleven.

After many years of hard work Welling were given senior status and were now trying to refurbish Bexley United's old Park View Road stadium. Bexley were now not competing at senior level and eventually Welling were given the all-clear to enter the Athenian League playing at Park View Road.

So that following Saturday my girlfriend Linda and I turned up at Park View Road to watch Welling play Edgware Town. I was taken aback at the superb condition of the pitch. Dartford had always been a bumpy surface. The ground looked a picture on this beautiful summer day.

We made our way into the bar after watching Welling win 3-1. Graham wandered in about 15 minutes later with a big smile on his face.

He sat himself down next to us and said: "Did you enjoy that?" I said 'Yes'. He asked if we could talk in private. I told my girlfriend I wouldn't be long and I was happy to follow Graham because the less my girlfriend knew about my finances the better!

I sat down opposite Graham in his office. He looked at me and said: "What's on your mind?"

"You know I would love to have you here".

I said I was flattered by his remarks but to be fair I had to tell him I was also talking with Dulwich Hamlet and Carshalton, and that they had both offered to meet the wages I was earning at Dartford which was £40 per week plus £10 appearance money.

Hurriedly he said: "OK we will give you £50 per week as well as a £500.00 signing on fee".

I had earned myself quite a reputation as a player at that time and I could see Graham was desperate to sign me. I was glad my girlfriend was not party to these negotiations because her eyes would have lit up when he mentioned the signing on fee.

I told Graham I would call him on Monday with a definite answer. We shook hands and said our goodbyes. I went back to the bar to get my girlfriend she said: "Did you sign?"

I replied: "No I told him I would ring him on Monday with an answer".

I talked with my girlfriend on the way home and remarked I wasn't keen on dropping down from the Southern League to the Athenian League. She said brutally: "Well Dartford don't want you. You're too old!"

Welling's offer of a signing-on fee was very tempting. Carshalton and Dulwich Hamlet were very good Isthmian League sides. Dulwich was only around the corner - literally. Their manager Jimmy Rose phoned me that Saturday night and asked me had I given his offer of £30 per week and a guaranteed place in the side any thought.

On impulse I said: "Yes Jim, I have given it a lot of thought, but I have decided to sign for Welling United."

He wished me luck but I could tell in his voice he was disappointed with my decision.

I told my girlfriend that I had decided to sign for Welling United and on the Monday I rang Graham to tell him the news. He was absolutely delighted. He then told me could I come to the ground on Tuesday evening when they trained to sign the necessary forms and meet a few of the players.

That Tuesday evening I met Graham in the bar and he laid out the forms for me to sign. He had invited the local press to take photos of me signing for the club and there was a quick interview with the local paper's sports journalist where I said all the right things about how impressed I was with the club's ambitions.

At around 8:15pm the players started to file into the bar having finished training. Graham asked them to sit down so that he could introduce the club's latest signing. I had been sat at a table in the corner. I could sense the players' curiosity as to who this guy was. Graham called me forward and said: "Fellas, I want to introduce you to Tommy Sampson who has joined us tonight."

I have to admit I didn't know many of the players, having spent five years at Dartford and not really following Welling at all. The only player I knew of was goalscoring sensation John Bartley.

I met the captain, midfielder Ray Burgess. If I am being truthful most of the players knew of me rather than knew me. In truth, it was a bit of a coup Graham getting me to sign for Welling. He asked me to come to training on Thursday night because I would be making my debut at home to Basildon this Saturday. He then pulled me into his office and handed me an envelope with my signing on fee of £500.

I tucked it into my back pocket and went back into the bar to chat to the players.

I left the ground at about 8:45pm to drive home to Peckham which took about 30 minutes. Opening my front door I went straight to the store cupboard where I kept my golf clubs. I took the envelope out of my back pocket and tucked it down in the side pocket of my golf bag. I went in the front room. "How did it go?" Linda asked.

"Fine" I said.

"I am playing Saturday. We're at home to Basildon."

It was about now that I thought about getting a job. I scanned all of the local papers for a sensible job that would fit in with my football. As luck would have it, I applied for a job with Lambeth Council as a courier driver.

I started on my first day and realised what a cushy number I had landed. The job involved picking up boxes of mail and dropping them at various offices around the borough. My co-worker was a chain-smoking middle-aged man called Peter Parsons. He had been working for the council for 25 years and knew all the shortcuts and little scams.

The vehicle I was using was an Austin mini-van which was great fun to drive. I was based in Brixton at Lambeth Town Hall. I was now driving a Morris Marina and the journey to Brixton took about 25 minutes. When I got there I would park in the council workers only car park. I would finish my job at 4:45pm each day. On a Tuesday and Thursday night (training nights) that would leave an hour or so to get to Welling.

I knew every short-cut through Eltham and Blackfen to get me there on training nights on time. I had a real thing about punctuality. Working for the council was getting me £13,000 per year so with my football money I was getting about £300 per week. Nice work if you can find it I thought to myself.

FROM THE DEN TO WEMBLEY

By now it was March 1981. Only three weeks after I had started working for Lambeth Council the Brixton Riots kicked off. On that first afternoon when the police ordered all the staff in the town hall to go home, I walked across the road to get to my car to drive home. I unlocked the barrier and looked up to see the car next to mine upturned.

I looked around and thought: "Fuck me, I'd better get out of here." I pulled out of the car park and turned left to go home. When I got to the end of the road there were about 40 guys just hanging around.

Turning left again into Coldharbour Lane I drove past two dark coloured coaches filled with police in riot gear. It was OK now I was out of Brixton heading for Camberwell and Peckham and home.

When I got in it was all over the news, showing police defending themselves against loads of guys throwing stones and bottles and any thing they could lay their hands on. As the night went on it gradually worsened the 10 o'clock news showed Brixton ablaze. I went to bed wondering whether to go to work in the morning.

I did, and driving through the back streets of Brixton I saw burnt-out buildings, piles of rubble and burnt out cars. Dustbins were strewn across the road. I was glad the weekend was almost upon us because as soon as it was here I could relax and think about my debut.

When Saturday came round I went through my normal routine: A big fried breakfast, cornflakes and the Daily Mail. Come 12:15, suited and booted, it was in the car and drive to Welling, aiming to arrive for 1:45. The players had been told to be in the dressing room for 2pm. I knew I would be early. I just loved to soak up the atmosphere of being inside the ground before kick-off.

That first three points was the only thing anyone thought about. We had a really good training session on

Thursday and I had got to know a lot of the players. I was going to play in the centre of the defence alongside centre half Nigel Ransom. He was a big character in the club and very soon we formed a solid partnership. We won the game 2-1 thanks to a John Bartley double. I had heard a lot about John in previous seasons and to watch him in person was a sight to see. The Park View Road pitch was every bit as good as I hoped. The attendance was a healthy 250. Nigel and I performed really well. I was really impressed with us as a team, I saw the Gaffer Graham as a willing amateur. The club was a family run club with Graham as manager and brother Barrie was the secretary, dad Sid was the chairman, Graham's wife Pam washed the kit. The club also had an excellent youth team set up.

Just before the season ended Graham resigned as manager. I thought that was a shame because we had done OK. Just after I had signed I had persuaded Graham to sign two old pals from Dartford who were being released. Centre forward John Mitchell and the very experienced and cultured ex-West Ham midfielder Kenny Wallace. John and Kenny were being released because, like me, they were supposedly past their sell by date. Both players made a big impression.

During that 81/82 season, a sixth place finish doesn't tell the full story. When Graham quit I went to his brother Barrie to ask if I could be considered for the vacant post as manager. He gave me a very vague reply, leaving me feeling that they already had someone lined up. I wasn't wrong because within a week it was announced in a blaze of publicity that Gravesend & Northfleet manager Tony Sitford had taken the job on a full time basis.

I was amazed because he was a very successful manager there and performing in the Southern Premier League. So why would he want to drop down two levels? My answer to that question came when it was rumoured that Tony had signed a five year contract. I knew him vaguely because having played at their local rivals Dartford and having spoken to mates that had played for him, I knew him to be a strict disciplinarian and uncompromising character.

When pre-season came around Kenny, John and I weren't very sure of what to expect. I knew Tony was going to run us into the ground. We trained in Danson Park which was adjacent to the ground and, as usual, pre-season was taking place in blazing hot temperatures.

Tony had inherited a young willing side sprinkled with some experience in me John and Kenny. He'd also inherited John Bartley, a goal scoring phenomenon. I pulled Tony to see what he had in mind. He told me I would have to take a cut in my wages. He wanted me drop from £50 to £30 per week.

I went to see Sid the chairman and tell him if I wasn't going to receive the wages I was getting last season then I would be off. Eventually Tony relented and I agreed to accept £40 per week.

I wasn't being greedy, it was my pride and I knew that at 27 years of age I would struggle to get £50 anywhere else.

I could have quite easily dropped into the Kent League but again, having been a professional footballer and been a Southern League Premier player, my pride wouldn't let me and so it was that for the start of season 82/83.

John, Kenny and me were in the side for that season's opening game at home to Ilford and playing for them that day was ex "Dart" and great friend Ben Embery.

Ben had been signed by Roy Dwight from Gravesend & Northfleet to replace me at Dartford but as the fates had it Ben and I would play together in the heart of the defence. Ben and I became great friends and years later still are.

FROM THE DEN TO WEMBLEY

A John Bartley brace saw us 2-0 up at half time in the season opener against Ilford which was the final scoreline. Bartley was a freak of nature. Strong, quick and in the penalty area as cool as a cucumber. The club had enquiries from scouts all around the country. Results were good in the early weeks of the season which saw us in the top four by the end of September.

Tony called me into his office one training night to ask me if I wouldn't mind playing left back for a couple of games. I looked at him a little perplexed and asked why. He explained that he had young lad in the youth team who he wanted to give a game or two. He wanted to play him on the left side of a four. But as he was only 18 he thought my experience would help him.

"How good is he?" I asked Tony.

"You'll see on Saturday at home to Redhill." he replied.

"What's his name?" I enquired.

"Andy Townsend. His dad Don played for Charlton for many years."

I was now very curious about this kid I was going to play alongside this Saturday.

On Thursday Tony brought this scrawny young kid over to introduce to me. I looked at him and thought to myself: "I have seen more fat on a butchers pencil"

The other thing I noticed was that his hair was half way down his back. Tony was very kind and said to the lad: "Tom is very experienced and he will look after you this Saturday. He's been a good player for many years".

Come Saturday, I lined up at left-back with the youngster hugging the left touchline. Before too long Bartley put us 1-0 up. John Mitchell was playing as an old fashioned centre forward and was a great partner for JB. "Mitch" was a beast of a centre forward. His physical style of play was too much for defenders at this level.

Bartley took advantage of the havoc he was causing and added two more goals, seeing us to a comfortable 3-0 victory. As for young Andy, he more than looked the part. His first touch was excellent and his response to my promptings spot on. We were just too good for our opponents so it was difficult to assess his performance.

Andy stayed in the side and I stayed at left back. I prided myself on being a genuine two-footed footballer. All those afternoons I spent with Ned pinging balls at one another did not go to waste.

Andy was a great talent. I wondered how long it would be before we lost him to a bigger club. Not only was I helping him, but he was doing the same for me. I was enjoying my new freedom. Andy was keeping the opposition so busy it allowed me to get forward and join in the fun. Graham Hobbins was still around the club watching all of our games and even watching training.

One night there was a new face in the dressing room. Tony came in and introduced him:

"Guys, meet our new signing, Colin Ford. Colin has joined us from Gillingham and will make his debut on Saturday against Hoddesdon Town".

I pulled Tony and asked him about Colin.

"He's a right back" Tony replied. Fordy and I were to become very close, so close in fact that 17 years later he was my first team coach at Wembley.

I came into training one Tuesday evening in October 1981 to be told the club had sold John Bartley to Millwall for £12.000. I wasn't at all surprised. The season was only three months old and John had already scored 22 goals. I was a little bit sorry only because I knew we didn't have anybody in the club who could fill John's boots. I always felt that John Mitchell could score 20-plus goals, especially with young Mr Townsend supplying a steady stream of crosses.

Because of JB's departure we never threatened the top of the table. I was now pushing 28 and I was released because of "budgetary"concerns or so I was told.

FROM THE DEN TO WEMBLEY

John Mitchell - Doing what he did best, terrorising defenders

John Bartley

Me warming up at Dartford (left), receiving the Player of the Year award (right).

FROM THE DEN TO WEMBLEY

Dressing room celebrations. Winning promotion 95/96 back to the Southern Premier League with Dartford - far right Peter Reeves who's reward was the sack!

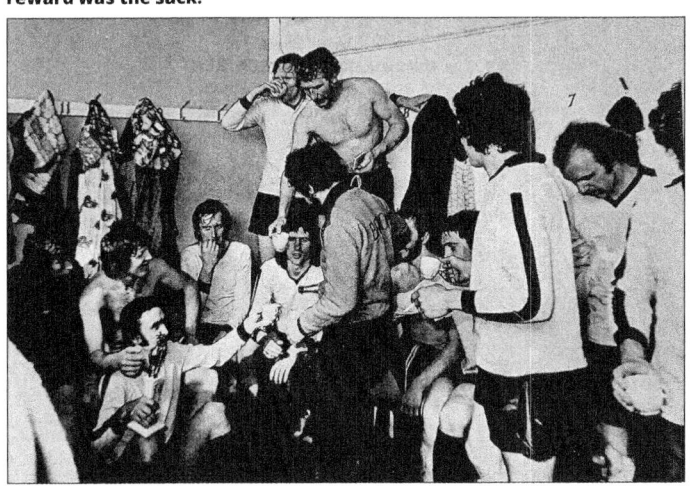

FROM THE DEN TO WEMBLEY

Kenny Wallace - Cultured Midfield player

Ben Embery

Andy Townsend - Talented youngster glad to have played a part in his story

Tony Sitford - Welling manager

7
BROMLEY-BOUND

In football, word of mouth was like a jungle telegraph, because within 48 hours of my leaving Welling my phone was red hot again. Jimmy Rose, who had tried to sign me for Dulwich Hamlet last season rang, as well as The Carshalton manager, Phil Amato who I had also turned down at the start of last season. The most interesting phone call came from Bromley's manager Phil Emblem.

I had a great friend of mine playing at Bromley top, goalscorer at all levels Phil Basey. Phil and I were pals having played against each other for many years. He had played for Hillingdon Borough and Maidstone United. We would chat away on the pitch and later on in the bar. Another mate of mine, ex-Spurs youth team coach Keith Waldon was there as well.

Emblem invited me to play in a pre-season friendly game at home to Midland League club Cradley Heath the following Saturday. I was really excited about linking up again with Keith and Phil.

That following Saturday I pulled into the car park at Hayes Lane, the home of Bromley Football Club.

I made my way into the dressing room where I met Phil Emblem and his first team coach Alan Hawkins.

Both were in their first managerial positions having both been players with the club. It was July 1982 and I was a month away from my 28th birthday and approaching 'veteran' status.

The dressing room door opened behind me and in walked Phil Basey and Keith Waldon. We sort of threw our arms around one another. Basey hadn't told me he was not playing up front anymore because of his age, and felt he had to drop back. He was now playing as a covering central defender off of the centre half. I thought: 'this is awkward, that's where I want to play!'

Emblem then said to me: "You're OK playing left-back aren't you Tom?"

"Yep, fine" I replied. It wasn't a problem for me. I had been playing there for Welling during the latter part of last season. Waldo was playing right back. I knew Keith because when I was at Dartford I had spent two months on loan at Sutton where he was also a right full-back. The Isthmian League was of the highest quality with teams like Enfield, Dagenham, Wycombe Wanderers, Leatherhead, Hendon and Dulwich Hamlet.

The game started and in those early minutes I felt very comfortable considering I'd done no pre-season training. I had this short lad playing left-side midfield outside of me. He had great skills and a terrific first touch. He was a joy to play with because I could give him the ball even when he was being shut down.

The guy's name was Dave Waight. We won the game comfortably and I knew walking off of the pitch this is the club where I wanted to play my football. I shook hands with Phil Emblem and Alan Hawkins and they seemed delighted with my performance. I sat down and chatted with Phil and Keith and asked what were Phil and Alan like as a management duo? Phil said: "OK, nothing special."

Emblem whispered to me that we'd have a chat outside when I'd showered. My girlfriend Linda was in the bar so I would go and get her when Phil and I had finished negotiating.

FROM THE DEN TO WEMBLEY

Emblem took me round the corner away from the dressing room and said to me: "I've got a very tight budget".

I had heard that one before I thought!

He asked me what sort of deal I was looking for. I said fifty pounds per week, and he came back straight away saying he could only afford £30. I said if he made it £40 I'd shake his hand.

"OK", he replied somewhat reluctantly, adding: "Don't tell your mates!" It was still 10 days to go before the opening game of the season against FA Trophy winners Bishops Stortford away.

We had some good players, especially the lad Waight and we also had this guy up front called 'Butch' Dunn. He was Bromley's own John Bartley. A prolific goalscorer.

We started the new season with a narrow 0-1 defeat at Stortford. At this time in my career I had fallen in love with the non-league game. At the turn of the year Phil resigned as manager, results weren't good and we were languishing in the lower half of the table. It all came crashing down for Phil when we lost in the FA Cup to Southern League side Fareham town 1-5 at home. It must have been hard for him. He was Bromley through and through.

Whilst playing that season I had the privilege of appearing in the same side as ex-Charlton and Gillingham right winger Colin 'Paddy' Powell. Paddy was the best crosser of a football I ever saw.

After Phil left the club they appointed former Maidstone goalkeeper Barry Watling. This was a disaster for me as Watling immediately wanted me out. I was approaching 29 years of age. I was still enjoying my football, although my right knee was falling a victim to the dreaded osteoarthritis.

I would play a game then go home and lay in bed crying because the pain was so unbearable.

Over the next two years I would have at least five arthroscopies (keyhole surgery) on the knee. Eventually I had to have a total knee replacement. I was 30.

After leaving Bromley I had a season at Tooting and Mitcham. Watling and his Bromley team were struggling terribly at the bottom of the league. I played for Tooting at Bromley late in the season and our 2-0 win saw Bromley slip down into the bottom two. I took no pleasure in Bromley's plight because I enjoyed playing there with Phil, Paddy, Waighty and co.

Whilst playing for Bromley in central midfield as an emergency replacement one evening away to Leytonstone and Ilford I had the distinctly unpleasant task of playing against a certain Terry Hurlock. A beast of a midfielder . That was when I decided to call it a day.

The total knee replacement was calling me from a distance. I was 30, but looking back I wouldn't have changed one single moment.

FROM THE DEN TO WEMBLEY

Terry Hurlock - played against Terry with one good knee! That was enough for me

Phil Emblem - My manager at Bromley, good guy

Phil Basey - Prolific non league goal scorer and great friend

FROM THE DEN TO WEMBLEY

8
A NEW CHALLENGE

I didn't kick a football in anger for at least another two years. I thought that was it.

Then, one evening, I answered the phone to an old schoolboy friend of mine Andy Woolford. Andy and I had played for Kent County schoolboys together back in the day. He said to me Sheppey United were looking for a new manager so I've thrown your name at them and they want to talk to you.

I was keen. "When can I talk to them?" I asked.

"How about tonight! Can you be at the ground for 8:30?"

It was 7:45 so I jumped straight in my car, headed down to the M20 and was soon pulling into the club car park at Sheppey's Botany Road ground.

I had played here in pre-season friendlies and Kent Senior Cup matches. I made my way to the boardroom. On opening the door I found three middle-aged men staring at me from behind this great big mahogany table.

One of these got up and introduced himself as Peter Sharrock, chairman of the football club. He introduced the other two guys as vice-chairman Dave Witton and club president Vic Ward.

Peter asked me lots of questions about my career and what my ambitions were. I answered all the questions in great detail and explained that, as I could no longer play, I wanted to carry on and manage or coach. I told them I had many contacts in the game. I wanted them to know my standards and what I expected of my players.

Within 20 minutes I had been offered the job on a two year contract earning £150.00 per week.

Sheppey had been relegated from the Southern League the previous season, hence the vacant managers position. Mr Sharrock gave me the name and address of a man called Keith Lissenden who had helped out running the first team and reserve team in the past couple of seasons. He gave me directions to Keith's house.

He said: "I will ring him and tell him you are coming to see him. I think he will prove invaluable to you." Peter was spot on with that one!

I was 37 years of age and finally back in the game. Ten minutes later I was sitting in Keith's front room drinking a cup of tea. He was a soft-spoken guy with what appeared to be a placid temperament.

We spoke about the job. He told me several players of last season's campaign had left the club, but there was the basis of the reserve team still around.

I asked Keith if he would be my assistant manager. I'd only just met him and it was a real gamble but it turned out to be the best decision I ever made.

I left Keith's house around 9:30pm armed with a raft of telephone numbers, mostly reserve team players from last year. Over the next couple of days and evenings, I phoned all of the numbers inviting them to pre-season training which would begin the following Saturday. I got a positive response from everyone (or so I thought!).

Keith met me at the ground on Saturday morning to await the players to arrive for our pre-season training. We waited and waited and by midday we had eight players in the dressing room. I asked Keith where everybody was. He just shrugged his shoulders.

I went into the dressing room and asked: "Where is everyone?"

"Why should we help you out?' You're only going to

use us until you bring your own players in". Came a reply.

He was right. That was exactly what I was going to do.

The season was just over a month away. I told Keith to leave it with me. That afternoon I got on the phone to every player I could think of. During my early retirement, I was helping my old boss Tony Sitford who was managing Corinthians FC as coach. I didn't do Tony any favours when I pinched several players from his team, including the exciting young centre forward Steve Hearn. My ex-Welling teammate Colin Ford was playing at Leyton Wingate and also decided to jump aboard the Tommy Sampson Sheppey United train.

A big mate of mine a guy called Harry Richardson was managing Kent League club Alma Swanley and I knew a number of his players from my days at Welling. Much to his disgust I nicked several of his squad too.

By Sunday evening I had about 13 players ready to start pre-season training the following Tuesday night. Almost all of the players I had recruited had a pal they thought would be good enough to play Kent League football. I phoned Keith and told him of my recruitment spree.

I was so relieved about the situation because of the promises I had made to the chairman Peter Sharrock. Keith had persuaded a couple of the better reserve team players to turn up, so with a group of about 16 training I felt much more positive about the situation.

I distinctly remember saying to Keith: "I bet Alex Ferguson doesn't have these problems". The only negative in all of this was I probably wouldn't get a Christmas card from Tony and Harry! Still, I was a manager now. It was dog eat dog.

I got busy organising pre- season friendlies. I managed to get Dartford to play us as well as the ambitious

Sittingbourne. A couple of the pals brought down by the guys I had recruited turned out to be decent and had a bit of pedigree. I also got lots of recommendations for players from local Kent managers, youth team players or more experienced lads who were looking for a fresh start.

One of these more experienced lads was a guy called Martin Farnie who had won the Kent League whilst playing for Tunbridge Wells. Martin was about to sign for Greenwich Borough but I managed to persuade him to sign for me. Martin had been around the Kent League for a few seasons and his knowledge would be invaluable. Whilst dealing with Greenwich Borough over Martin, their manager asked me would I want to take his centre forward off of his hands?

I was fortunate to have a good playing budget, so I could pay players decent money as well as travel expenses so that obviously made it easier for me to get players to sign.

Now back to that Greenwich Borough centre forward, a lad called Paul Kenny - 'Badger' to his friends, don't ask me why. Paul came with a health warning. He was a complete maverick, turning up for games at 2 o'clock, missing training and getting sent off.

I asked Martin what I should do with him. He replied: "Tom, sign him. He will get you twenty goals."

I did sign Paul but not before I took him out for a pint and laid down the law, telling him: "The first time you let me down, you are out". I gambled with Paul, paying him over the odds and £10 for every goal he scored - out of my own pocket I hasten to add!

Our first pre-season friendly was against Spartan League Waltham Abbey. On a scorching-hot July Saturday afternoon Badger came good, scoring two goals in our 3-0 victory as well as endearing himself to the 300-plus supporters. Three weeks prior to this game I had eight people turn up for the start of pre-season training and I felt I was allowed to bask in a little bit of the glory that was hopefully coming my way.

Next up was Southern League Dartford the following Tuesday evening and a 5-1 win had the supporters talking about getting promoted back to the Southern League at the first time of asking. I tried to dampen their expectations but it reached fever pitch a week later in the local Swale derby against Sittingbourne for our last pre-season friendly.

In front of 500 supporters, Badger scored a last minute screamer from 20 yards out to see us win 5-4.

Fordy and Martin were playing their part in pulling this Ragbag Rovers together. Expectations were high and trying to manage them wasn't easy. But those expectations were fuelling the feelgood factor around the place.

The local sports editor for the local rag was an ex-Sheppey player called Micky Rees. I was bigging the team up now. Mick had a fearsome reputation as a tough tackling centre half. It was the one position I hadn't quite filled so I invited him to train with us to see if he could get himself fit enough to play again. After a couple of sessions Mick told me: "I am ready whenever you need me".

The fixtures were released and as Sod's Law would have it, our first game was at home to Alma Swanley, Harry Richardson and all.

Mick was training well but with only two weeks to that opening game I was keeping my options open. The only position I was struggling for was goalkeeper. I mentioned this to Mick and he came back to me.

"No problem, my brother Mark is a great 'keeper. He's already played for Faversham and Sittingbourne". A little sceptical, I asked him to bring him to training the following Thursday.

On that Thursday training night, I put on a shooting session, just to have a look at Mark. He looked the part, making his fair share of great saves and when the session finished I took him aside and we shook hands on £50 per week and £5 for every clean sheet he kept (out of my pocket again).

For the Tuesday before our opening game I arranged a home friendly with Isthmian League Division One team Whyteleafe. Three goals from my young central striker, a boy called Steve Hearn, prompted a £3,000 bid from the opposing manager, ex-Crystal Palace man Paul Hinshelwood.

I let Paul talk to Steve but as Steve didn't drive he turned their offer down. I was delighted because Steve and Badger made a dream pairing and I could see them terrorising Kent League defences next season.

The previous month's stressful goings on taught me so much. From chasing players to shambolic training sessions. I was in no doubt how hard it would be to bring success back to the club and realised very quickly that for players to reach the standards I was going to set would mean making compromises.

Managing part-time players was going to test me and if I didn't learn quickly I would lose their loyalty and commitment. Pre-season had actually gone *too* well, because the expectations of everyone around the place were now sky high.

I was flattered by all the attention I was receiving. My reputation had gone before me, playing in some great sides and achieving success as a player had left me a lot to live up to.

That first season at Sheppey was a rollercoaster. After nine games we were third-bottom of the league and then our tenth game saw us lose at home to bottom-placed Darenth Heathside. I was very despondent. I had a conversation with the chairman later that evening and foolishly offered my resignation. Fortunately he would have none of it and told me what a good job I was doing in difficult circumstances.

I breathed a huge sigh of relief but despite poor results I was still confident I could turn things around. When I told Keith what I had done he looked at me and said: "You prat! You are exactly what this club needs".

The Saturday after that disastrous Heathside defeat we were at home to Tony Sitford's Corinthians in a Kent Senior Trophy tie and with the game finely poised at 0-0 with barely three minutes to go, a harmless left-wing cross from us was headed into his own net from about twelve yards by a Corinthian defender. After ten games without a win this was an outrageous piece of luck and lifted everybody from the gloom and doom that had surrounded the club.

That piece of good fortune turned our season around and although I wasn't to know it, for another 18 years altered my career path. The big teams in the Kent League at that time were money-laden Herne Bay and Faversham Town. They were fighting it out at the top of the table whilst we were struggling in the bottom three. That victory over Corinthians saw us go on a 32-game unbeaten run in the league which had Faversham and Herne Bay looking over their shoulders.

Steve Hearn and Badger were enjoying themselves immensely but unfortunately I had to release Paul Kenny in January for disciplinary reasons. When Steve Hearn first came to the club he brought with him his mate Terry Nightingale. A raw, lightning-quick right-winger.

As luck would have it my centre-half Martin Osbourne was a prison officer working at Swaleside Prison on the island and he recommended a lad doing time for a minor offence.

He said: "If I can get him out on special leave this Saturday you could give him a game and see if you can use him".

It was certainly one of my more unusual transfer deals!

We were due to play Slade Green at home. The terms of this lad's release meant he was in Martin's custody and had to be back inside by 5pm on the Saturday. Martin turned up with this scruffy scrawny looking lad who he introduced to me as Mark Dryden. I led him into my office for a quick chat. "Where do you want to play?" I asked.

"Left wing" he replied confidently. I took him back into the dressing room to clarify to the players where Mark was going to play and how we were going to set up.

I had decided on a whim to give Steve's mate Terry Nightingale a game too. It was quite the gamble. Here I was hoping to climb further up the league and keep this incredible unbeaten run going and giving debuts to two lads I had never seen play before!

Having released Badger it left Steve up the middle on his own. I was making it up as I went along. We were going to go with a 4-3-3 leaving Dryden out left Hearn up the middle and Nightingale wide right.

We kicked off and inside 15 minutes I had made my mind up about both Dryden and Nightingale. They were very quick and exciting to watch. We won the game very comfortably 3-0 which took us into the top four. The paying public were loving it because my team was a breath of fresh air.

After having endured last season's relegation campaign, I was basking in the adulation, not daring to tell them the chaos and good-guessing going on behind the scenes. We were close to breaking the Faversham/Herne Bay monopoly at the top of the table.

I was hearing rumours that Sheppey were in so much debt that it was likely the Botany Road Stadium would have to be sold. With a couple of games of the season to go we were due to play Herne Bay away. 'The Bay' needed every point available to beat Faversham to the league title. We went there and turned in a scintillating performance to win 2-0 with both Nightingale and Dryden scoring. It had been eight years since I had dropped out of the Football League and my stock in the non-league world was very high.

After the Herne Bay game I was approached by their manager Trevor Gowan who told me he had offered his resignation to his chairman earlier in the week, citing business and family reasons for not being able to carry on as manager next season.

"Do you want me to throw your name in the hat for the job?" he asked me.

"Yes, absolutely" I said immediately.

I realised that Sheppey were in debt which would leave me and my team high and dry. Within a couple of days I received a call from Herne Bay's 25-year old chairman Michael Todd: "I understand you're interested in becoming our next manager?"

I confirmed that I was and told him about my situation at Sheppey. I was out of contract. When it became known that the Herne Bay job was up for grabs, there was a local media frenzy with all sorts of names being thrown about.

I asked the chairman if he wanted to meet up and chat, I wanted him to approach my current club officially for permission to speak to me. I felt so strongly about my allegiance to Sheppey and I wouldn't be comfortable going behind their back. After all, they gave me my first break in management.

A few days after my telephone conversation with their chairman, Herne Bay won the league over Faversham under an interim manager. My Sheppey team finished third. I was really proud of that achievement especially as we were in the bottom three after nine games. Keith Lissenden played a huge part in that fantastic season. He was so calm and understated, keeping my feet on the ground when I started to get ahead of myself.

I met with Michael Todd and his father Bob who was vice-chairman. I pointed out that despite being champions there were a few players I didn't fancy, as well as making it clear that I would be bringing players in from Sheppey United. They promised not to interfere. Music to any manager's ears, but a hard promise to keep!

At the end of that meeting they offered me the job. I informed Sheppey of my decision immediately. Peter Sharrock was very kind, thanking me for the great job I had done. In turn I recommended my replacement. A guy who I played veterans football with: John Roseman. John was also good friends with Colin Ford who had been my captain and at 30 years old knew all the players.

Keith was coming to Herne Bay with me so it seemed sensible that Colin stay with John. Peter heeded my advice and at the end of that week both Sheppey and Herne Bay had new management teams in place.

I signed a two year contract. I was on a high, but, as is so often the case, life brought me back to down earth with a bump and put mere football into perspective with the news that my wife Carole had been diagnosed with breast cancer.

On the first night of pre-season training at Herne Bay prior to the 93/94 season, I released seven players, sure in the knowledge that I was bringing better players in from my last club.

It goes without saying those conversations weren't pleasant. But that was me all over, direct and single-minded. I had also brought Martin Farnie with me from Sheppey as first team coach. Martin and I had become very close during that one season and because Keith was so placid and studious I needed Martin with me because he was very frank and forthright. I needed someone to back me up in what was going to be a hostile dressing room.

The players I had left were very cynical about me. I could understand that because I had broken up a side that had been together for three years. Very soon after those early pre-season sessions I started to bring in players from Sheppey, trying to find a nice balance. As champions last season Herne Bay had been a bog standard 4-4-2 whereas I was committed to a 5-3-2 set up.

Pre-season was difficult because trying to teach old dogs new tricks was proving problematic. Eventually we were ready to go and by coincidence, just as at Sheppey United, we were due to host Alma Swanley who were going to make it very difficult for us for no other reason than Herne Bay's manager was Tommy Sampson!

That 93/94 season turned out to be a record-breaking one. We won the Kent League championship by an incredible 25 points. You may think because of that winning margin the competition was weak. In truth it was a brutal league because everyone we played were so determined to upset our apple cart and along with that I had made myself very unpopular because I was prone to bigging my team and myself up to such a point it got on people's nerves.

I was desperately disappointed when the chairman told me they couldn't afford the money needed to achieve the required ground grading and get automatic promotion to the Southern League. That summer saw Margate and Folkestone approach Herne Bay for permission to speak to me about their clubs' vacant managerial posts.

The club's response to those enquiries was to offer me a four-year contract worth £20,000 per year. The chairman and his father promised me that if, in that four year term, we were to win another title, the ground would be upgraded to the necessary standard and promotion would be a given.

I signed the contract which would take me through to the 98/99 season. During those four campaigns we won the title in 96/97 which included a domestic treble of the league, League Cup, and Senior Trophy - a feat never achieved before. Again, I was told the ground did not meet the grading requirement.

I was devastated because it was obvious to me that I'd had the wool pulled over my eyes. That aside I was becoming to be known as a serial winner. The following season I decided to carry on convincing myself we would have a real crack at the Carlsberg FA Vase. I really believed we were good enough to get to Wembley.

What a way to finish I thought.

I put this to the guys and we all agreed that would be our focus. Sitting at home a few days into the New Year, my fax machine started rumbling. I tore the sheet from the machine and reading it I was gobsmacked:

"DEAR TOM." WE ARE INFORMING YOU THAT THE TODD FAMILY WILL NO LONGER BE THE CLUB'S MAIN SPONSOR AS OF THE 30th MARCH 1998."

It went on to say that as of the 1st April 1998 I would no longer be under contract to Herne Bay Football Club and therefore will be a free agent from that date onwards.

FROM THE DEN TO WEMBLEY

The fax was signed chairman Michael Todd. I showed my wife Carole who, because of her cancer diagnosis was enduring chemotherapy and radiotherapy sessions at the Royal Marsden Hospital in Kensington west London. Technically I still had one year left on my contract which meant, give or take a few pounds, I was owed a minimum of £18,000. I was, in effect, my wife's main carer. So my wages from Herne Bay was a large and a significant chunk of what we needed to live on. The next three months went along as normal. Everybody in the non-league world was speculating where I would end up.

Me signing my contract at Herne Bay. Michael Todd ,Chairman (left) Vic Chairman, Bob Todd (father)

Harry Richardson - I nicked a couple of his players, he did'nt send me a christmas card for the next ten years. A legendary Kent football character. Loved him dearly.

FROM THE DEN TO WEMBLEY

Me with the Kent Senior Trophy, Kent League Cup and Kent League Trophy - an unprecedented treble in 1996/97

Celebrating another good win

9
A GOOD DEAL

Unbeknown to me, a local wealthy businessman from Walmer near Deal had become the new owner and chairman of Deal Town Football Club with big ideas to develop their stadium. Apparently he was willing to invest £750,000 to develop the ground so it could be used by the local community.

Some time during those first three months of the season I received a call from Deal Town's manager Dave Dadd who told me his new chairman and owner Roy Smith would like to talk to me about the managers position.

I was confused because, as far as I knew, Dadd was still the charge. Dave told me he was going to stand down because he had recommended me to be the new manager. Dave arranged for me to meet Smith at his home later the following week. We chatted and he explained his ambitions for the football club.

He wasn't interested in winning the Kent League, he wanted to build a new main stand facility which could be used by the community. Inside this facility would be a large function room and a small gymnasium. Through his lawyers, Smith was fighting for planning permission.

When I questioned what he wanted from me if he didn't want me to be successful on the pitch, he explained that he wanted me to raise the profile of the club. We parted company and agreed to meet up and talk again the following week.

The next day I arranged to meet Michael and Bob Todd at their office a minute or so from the ground. I informed them I was talking to Deal Town. We were in the first week of April so I felt it was the right thing to do to let them know. I also reminded both of them that they owed me £18,000 for the last year of my contract. They both raised their eyebrows and invited me to sit down.

I won't go into detail but I left their office 45 minutes later and got into my car with a huge grin all over my face.

Roy called me to arrange to meet a few days later. He asked me to bring my current Herne Bay contract with me. I met with Smith early the following week at his house and he explained again his ambitions for the club and the team. He asked to see my Herne Bay contract worth £18,000 per year and said: "I will give you an extra £10,000 if you accept the manager's job". I didn't need asking twice!

We shook hands and then he led me into another reception room where we sat down and he passed me the new contract to read and sign. An announcement would be made to the press the following day.

I drove home excited by the prospect of what was in store. Herne Bay had appointed reserve team manager Jeff Record as first team manager and his first task was to tell the players that because of the club's financial position now that the Todd family had pulled their sponsorship from the club they were all free agents and could leave the club immediately. This was the only option open to Jeff had as the club had no funds to pay the wages.

During the summer of 1998 I signed all twelve players that Herne Bay released. It was now 24 years since I'd left Millwall, but I still clung on to those professional standards that I learned back then. Those standards made me a target for the many cynical non-league people. My players would turn up to all games in a shirt and tie and I would arrive in a sharp suit. My fellow non-league managers would invariably turn up in jeans or work overalls. I felt we had to set ourselves apart from the rest, I wanted to intimidate my opposition.

In doing so I made myself a hate figure. I took my fair share of stick from opposition fans and even players. My wife Carole had passed away, but before she died she made me promise to carry on with my football. I therefore felt an added impetus and inspiration taking up the reins at the start of each season.

My first match as Deal Town manager was away to Whitstable Town which we drew 2-2. My team was full of ex-Herne Bay players and initially the Deal supporters were reluctant to throw their full support behind their new team. This reluctance turned into apathy, which is never a good atmosphere between team and fans. The local paper even received letters from irate supporters arguing that this new manager had destroyed their beloved club. I tried to pacify these fans by addressing their grievances in my programme notes.

Over the last few seasons Deal Town had always been the proverbial bridesmaids, scoring hundreds of goals - but conceding almost as many. I was desperate to change this but it was obviously going to take time. Keith and I found ourselves placating supporters in the bar after games because we didn't play the 'Deal way'.

It's fair to say that previous Deal Town teams had been known for their attractive style of football but I was more of a pragmatist. I had won Kent League titles playing high-tempo football, suffocating the life out of the opposition. I felt that the supporters were living in the past and hoped that it would only take a couple of those scintillating performances we were capable of producing to get them back onside.

That performance came when we dismantled Hythe Town 6-1 with the summer's marquee signing Welsh international and Gillingham record-goalscorer Steve Lovell getting a hat-trick. Suddenly gates were increasing as word-of-mouth was getting my players their just rewards. That first season saw us finish runners-up to local rivals Ramsgate. I wasn't that surprised because of the early season turmoil. We did however win the League Cup beating Crayford-based VCD Athletic 1-0.

During the 1999/2000 pre-season I signed a couple of players that I'd had on my wish list for a couple of seasons who deserve a mention. Firstly Millwall nut Jamie Kempster from Greenwich Borough and also from 'The Borough', the cultured Philip Turner. We had an unbelievably strong squad for that Level.

I spent many evenings with Keith watching all sorts of games. Keith would make copious notes, he was a real student of the game. I couldn't have wished for a better right-hand man. I had also managed to persuade Colin Ford to join me as first team coach. During that 1999/2000 season, I ran two Deal Town Soccer Schools during the holidays.

The uptake was truly astonishing and we had, during the two weeks that the soccer school ran, over 120 girls and boys participate. This was the ideal opportunity to mend fences with the Deal public. It was also another revenue stream. All through that season Roy was being thwarted by Dover District Council's reluctance to grant him planning permission. It was costing the chairman thousands of pounds in legal fees. All he wanted to do was spend £750,000 of his own money on building a new 500-seater stand facility with function and meeting rooms that could be hired out to the community for various reasons.

Roy's vision was to see the football club become self sufficient. He was an outspoken man and said it as he saw it, which almost certainly went against him in negotiations with the council. In the meantime, the first team were flying high in the league and finally winning over the Deal public.

My personal stock with the supporters was also on the up.

The team were just too well organised and professional for the rest of the league. There wasn't any team that could go toe-to-toe with us, and if any team tried to there was only one ending. The team I sent out most weeks were just too strong for our opposition.

It was now an incredible 25 years since I had left Millwall. My journey through the non-league football world had taken in over 200 games for Dartford, 80-odd games for both Welling and Bromley, and three Kent League titles in five years as manager at Herne Bay including 14 Manager of the Month awards. A humble but decent career.

Veteran signing Steve Lovell was proving to be a great role model for my younger players. When I signed him from Tonbridge Angels the previous summer I tried to sell him the FA Vase and Wembley dream. I picked his very knowledgeable brain on many occasions and I will never forget him playing for me at Greenwich Borough one Saturday. Borough had a big left-footed centre-half called Paul Collins. It was windy and the pitch as bumpy as the surface of the Moon. We drew 0-0 and Paul had lumped Steve all over the place. I got in the dressing room and said to him: "Welcome to my world!"

He looked me straight in the eye and said: "I loved every minute of it!"

Fair play I thought. The guy's clearly a pro.

FROM THE DEN TO WEMBLEY

10
THE ROAD TO WEMBLEY

The FA Vase was becoming something of an obsession for me.

It was all very well and good winning Kent League titles, but it was small potatoes compared to a Wembley appearance. We were going along nicely in the domestic scene but when the secretary told me we had been drawn away to ambitious Wessex League team Eastleigh in the first round proper I asked my youth team manager, former Ashford Town legendary goalkeeper Peter Carman, if he would go and do a report on them for me.

The following Sunday morning after he had watched our opponents, I went to watch the youth team play. Peter and I chatted after the game and he gave me the report he'd compiled on them. We were due to play them in late October which gave me about three weeks to digest Peter's comprehensive findings.

The players were under no illusion as to what this competition meant to me. When the day came we set off around the M25 and down the M3 to Eastleigh. We were within ten minutes of our opponents' ground when our coach driver took a wrong turn, sending us through narrow country lanes. It didn't help that it was chucking it down with rain. We finally arrived at the ground twenty minutes late. The teamsheet had to be in by 2:30. By the time I took it to the referee, apologising profusely for it not being in on time, it was 2:45.

Colin and Keith were giving the players their final instructions. I got into the dressing room just as my captain Terry Martin was leading the lads out. I looked at Colin and Keith and said: "Everything done?" "Yes, all done." They said in unison. I hated not delivering those final instructions but the circumstances of the day so far meant that could not happen and the beauty of having Keith and Colin was I could trust them to follow my instructions to the letter.

The three of us made our way to the dugout. It was still pissing down with rain. The first ten minutes I was studying Eastleigh closely to see if Peter had got it right and we opened the scoring after eleven minutes, but by half time we were 1-3 down.

As the three of us walked towards the away team dressing room I felt my temper start to boil over.

I slammed the dressing room door shut behind me and positioned myself deliberately behind this old fashioned medical table. It had a fragile vinyl covering. Looking straight ahead I slammed my hand down on it saying aggressively: "If you all think I am going out of this fucking competition before the end of fucking October you got another think coming!"

Every time I slammed my hand down on this old table dust flew up in front of my eyes!

I made two substitutions quickly and sent them out into the rain with my last rant wringing in their ears: "Don't you dare come back without a good result." It wasn't a very constructive half time team talk but I got it out of my system. Remarkably we won 4-3 and were into the second round proper. After the game I got slaughtered for my 'ridiculous and pointless half time rant'.

Captain Terry Martin came up to me in the bar after the game and said to me: "That was premeditated wasn't it?" I had huge respect for Terry, he had been my captain at Sheppey, Herne Bay and now Deal. I simply replied to Terry: "You are probably the only player here except Steve Lovell that would have used the word premeditated! "

Colin and I sat together on the coach home when, ten minutes into our journey the chairman popped his head around the seat.

"Fellas, we dodged a bullet today!" he beamed.

Roy was a great chairman to work for. He never interfered and always had a word of encouragement for me. He also wanted to know what players I was looking to bring into the club. He had very high standards.

During that season Roy and I played a lot of golf together along with Dave Dadd, who was now stadium manager. Whilst Roy was a very wealthy man you would never have guessed, it he was a laconic character.

After the "Miracle of Eastleigh" we all eagerly awaited our draw for the next round on the following Monday lunchtime and I jumped onto the FA website to check. I scrolled down the page where I found Deal Town vs East Preston. I knew they were a Sussex County League side. I phoned my secretary to ask him to find out their upcoming fixtures.

I wanted to watch them play at home where they would be at their strongest. The secretary came back to me with their fixtures. The only home game I could get to was a Tuesday evening. I told the chairman and he said: "I've got an idea, we'll find a golf course nearby, play 18 holes, have something to eat and go watch the game".

In past seasons I would have had Keith for company on these scouting missions. I explained to Keith what the chairman had suggested because I knew he would be disappointed at not casting an eye over our next opponents. The chairman also invited Dave Dadd. He was a retired firefighter and a lifelong Deal Town fan. On the day of our scouting mission we set off before lunch to make our way to the golf course we had booked. We teed off and I couldn't but help but think what a favour Michael and Bob Todd at Herne Bay had done me by sending me that fax in the first few days of 1998.

After the three of us had finished we ate our dinner in the clubhouse. East Preston's ground was a two minute drive away from the golf course. Armed with my pen and notepad, we all settled down to watch our next Vase opponents.

The game was still three weeks away and would be up against Scotland vs England on Television so naturally it would affect the gate. Come the day our opponents offered little resistance in our 3-0 victory so into the third round we sailed. On the following Monday I was in Norfolk playing golf with my golf society. I had invited Colin as my guest. The draw for the third round was being broadcast live on the FA website. Against all golfing etiquette I put my mobile in my golf bag because I had asked the chairman to text me or leave a voicemail as soon as he knew the draw. As we were about to start the back nine I heard my phone ping indicating a text. I apologised to my playing partners and looked at my phone to read the text Roy had sent: "Watton United at home". I had to admit I knew nothing about them.

When we'd finished I immediately looked up Watton's details only to find out they played in the United Eastern Counties League and were managed by former Cambridge United and Everton striker Alan Biley. They were lying fourth in their league after six matches.

As always I rang my secretary Colin Adams to ask him to obtain Watton's upcoming fixtures. I needed to see them away from home as near to our tie as possible which was coming up in a fortnight.

Their next away game was on a night we were due to play Beckenham Town away. I decided to go on my own to watch them, leaving Keith and Colin to run the

Beckenham game. Watton were playing Fakenham Town away, so off I went into the wilds of Norfolk to study our next Vase opponents.

I took notes for the whole 90 minutes. The following morning I transferred my almost illegible scribblings to a proper lined notepad. The following Thursday I gave Colin and Keith these notes so they could familiarise themselves with Watton United. During the Sheppey United and Herne Bay years and now Deal I never went into an important cup match without having watched our opponents, this meant Keith and I drove to all parts of the country gathering vital information.

We were in late November 2000 and the Vase game was to take place on December 4th. I always gave the players the basic information about our visitors. Coming in earlier than normal on the relevant Saturday, I always trusted my players to take on board the details I was giving them.

Watton stung us early on by taking the lead with a wicked deflection and we went in 0-1 down at half time which meant we had to stay calm and continue doing what we were good at. That was to keep getting the wing-backs forward and getting the ball into Steve Lovell's feet. I can't lie because of my obsession about Wembley I was unusually nervous taking my seat in the dugout at the beginning of the second half. I needn't have worried because on the hour my left wing-back Paul Ribbens got forward and cut inside, and from 18 yards drilled a powerful right-footed shot low into the bottom of the Watton net to make it 1-1. I jumped up as we all did. I then had that terrible pessimistic thought we could still lose this.

The last 30 minutes was mostly all us and as we got into the final ten minutes we forced several corners, the last one of four on the spin saw the ball fall to one of my 'wish list' players, the cultured Phil Turner and on the half turn he found the top corner. TWO-ONE - and into the fourth round!

250 Deal Town supporters celebrated outside our dressing for the next 15 minutes singing: "We're on our way to Wembley" I pushed Phil Turner out of the door to drink in the adulation that was coming his way. When he came back in his hair was all bedraggled where he had been the subject of his fans' celebrations and enthusiasm. Then I heard it, the fans singing: "There's only one Tommy Sampson"

I was humbled by that, but it would mean nothing if we didn't get to the 'holy grail' of football: Wembley Stadium.

The following Monday lunchtime I was listening to the FA website doing the fourth round draw live. I heard all the "big guns" come out. Bedlington, Taunton, Tiverton, Vauxhall Motors.

The draw seemed to go on forever with no sign of Deal Town. All I wanted to hear was us to come out first which obviously meant being at home. We were now only five games from the final including a two leg semi-final.

I lost concentration as the draw seemed to go on forever. Then I heard "Deal Town", but I missed who came out before us. I cursed quietly to myself and had to wait until the draw was recapped to find out we were away to Crook Town. I hastily picked up my non-league directory and quickly thumbed my way to Crook Town who played in the Arnott Insurance Northern League.

Crook was just north of Bishop Auckland so we were looking at an 800-mile round trip. I spoke to the chairman later that day and he casually remarked with that wicked sense of humour he possessed: "Shouldn't be a problem".

I said we'd have to stay overnight and he replied: "Leave It with me" Roy duly booked a beautiful hotel in Bishop Auckland for Friday and Saturday.

My one big headache was that our prolific midfield goalscorer Roly Graham's wife was due to give birth on the day of the game. After talking to Keith, Colin and Roly it was decided that Colin would drive Roly up on the Friday before the game. Roly would then stay with us on Friday night and straight after the game Colin would drive Roly home in my car.

I will always be indebted to Roly's wife Stephanie for allowing the him time off to come and play. I was scratching my head as to how to get to watch them play. The game was due to be played in late December. Roy asked me to find a hotel as near as I could,watch them and stay overnight, letting Keith and Colin take the league game at home to Slade Green.

We were top of the league, the points were vital and whilst I had complete faith in Keith and Colin, I just hated not being at our games. I booked a hotel in Darlington and asked my partner Sandie if she wanted to come with me. "Absolutely" she replied. I mean, a night in Darlington with me, how could she refuse?

On the Friday morning we set off for on the long drive north east. Arriving about 5:30pm, after settling in we asked the receptionist where the nearest Indian restaurant was and she handed me a card for The Sun Palace in Darlington town centre. We phoned to book a table and when we entered the restaurant we were amazed at the decor, it really was like a palace, and £65 later we made our way back to the hotel after having had the most fantastic Indian meal we'd ever had.

The following morning we drove into Bishop Auckland where Sandie proceeded to set my credit card alight in the retail centre. We were both wrapped up against the bitter January wind and after quenching Sandie's retail thirst we set off to watch Crook play Easington Colliery.

Crook's stadium was very old fashioned, a huge imposing wooden stand with open concrete terraces.

FROM THE DEN TO WEMBLEY

We took our seats at the very back of the old wooden stand, it was absolutely freezing. Trying to write notes was difficult because my hand very quickly got freezing cold.

The wind was blowing sideways across the pitch at about 30mph. Crook were a famous club in the north east having made several appearances at Wembley in the now defunct FA Amateur Cup.

Their most recent visit was in 1964 where in front of a capacity crowd they beat London team Enfield Town by two goals to one.

The game was uneventful. The wind was spoiling any chance of anybody playing any constructive football. I can honestly say that, apart from that Indian meal, the weekend was a waste of time.

When Sandie and I got back home on the Sunday I spoke to the chairman. I told him the weekend was not really very fruitful and he said to send Keith up again next week. Unlike me, Keith had a separate full time job - at the Docks on the Isle of Sheppey.

I rang him to ask if he could go and watch Crook the next weekend, telling him take his wife Judith to make a weekend of it and he agreed, as I knew he would.

Like me, Keith made for Darlington to his hotel on the Friday. That Saturday we were at home to my old team Sheppey United.

Just before the game started I got a call from Keith who told me Crook's game had been postponed because of a frozen pitch.

As I was standing in the middle of the dressing room when I got his call all the guys could hear what Keith was saying and in unison they let out a sarcastic roar. Keith said he was going over the road to watch them train. I told him to stay up another day and do some sightseeing.

Keith's loyalty to me was touching and his contribution to my career could not be underestimated. The chairman was a great man and would meet all of our expenses when on these scouting missions.

Keith would have been happy that we beat 'The Islanders' 1-0 with serial goalscorer Roly Graham smashing a late winner in off the crossbar.

We were now flying at the top of the league as well as being in the fourth round of the FA Vase. I couldn't help casting my mind back to when I joined the club and the suspicion and hostility towards me and my players

All that had changed and we were now idolised by the Deal faithful.

I had reached the fifth round once before with Herne Bay in 96/97 where we were beaten in controversial circumstances by Isthmian League team Banstead Athletic when they scored from an indirect free kick without any player touching the ball.

I believed that Herne Bay side were more than good enough to get to Wembley.

Six of that team started in the side that beat Watton so with 'only' Crook Town standing in our way of another fifth round appearance, I was at pains to leave no stone unturned.

Keith was with me at Banstead that day and I knew that he would have the same desire as me to go deeper into the competition.

The Vase was not just about winning a trophy, it was about playing at Wembley. Looking back I suppose my obsession with Wembley started with that Banstead defeat.

In the week before the Crook Town tie I signed a big centre forward from Ashford Town called Jon Warden. He'd had a terrific non-league career playing for the likes of Crawley Town and Kingstonian.

He was a powerful central striker and brought a physicality to his game that made most defenders tremble. I felt that Jon would be good cover for Steve Lovell for the last six weeks of the season.

It was at the end of a dreadful week of bad weather including driving snow blizzards and high winds that we left for Crook Town to play our fourth round tie. We were staying in a luxury hotel just outside Crook for both the Friday and Saturday night which was just as well. Because of the bad weather, our trip took nearly eight hours!

We arrived just in time for the players to shower and to have dinner. Luckily for us the chairman had hired a luxury coach for the journey with tea-making facilities and toilets. At about 8:30 Colin arrived with Roly. I got the kitchen to make them both a light supper. Normally Colin and I would room together, but as this was Jonny Warden's first trip I thought if he roomed with me I could give him the run down of the team and how we played. I made the decision to play Jon the following day instead of Steve Lovell who had taken the decision like a real pro. After all, I was asking him to travel almost 800 miles to sit on the bench and probably not kick a ball in anger. He also understood my decision to sign Jon.

Jon and I both showered and got dressed. Jon was 6 foot 2 inches and a big unit. Over dinner we chatted about what to expect tomorrow. Jon was a softly spoken man which belied his on-field hard man persona.

I woke early that next morning listening to gale force winds battering the hotel. We all met for breakfast at 10am. I had asked the hotel if I could use their small function room for one last de-briefing for the players.

In the room there was a flip chart I could use. On the second page of this chart I wrote in large block capitals the word "BOLLOCKS". Having finished my organising I called the players in to find a seat and listen. The chairman came in and took a seat as did local paper journalist Mike Green whom I had invited for the weekend to see how we go about things.

When everyone had settled I turned over the first page of that flip chart to let the players see the word I had written earlier. I detected a giggle from the room.

I turned around and gave them both barrels, jabbing my finger against the large black capital letters on the board: "That's it, you laugh, but if any one of you haven't got these this afternoon, you will be going out of this competition!"

It was quite an unexpected tirade, while outside, the stormy wind continued to batter the hotel.

At about 1:45pm we jumped on the coach to do the five minute journey to Crook's ground and the wind was still blowing at around 40mph. I spoke to my captain Terry Martin about the toss and we both walked to the centre spot where the wind was gusting straight down the ground from one goal to the other. I decided that if we won the toss we should defend the wind and have it at our backs in the second half. Terry agreed. I think he was happy that I'd made the decision for him. The decision paid off handsomely as we romped to a 3-0 victory. Father-to-be Roly Graham gave us a lead early into the second half (with the wind at our backs!).

Two very late goals from my lightning quick forward Steve Marshall gave the scoreline a misleading look. Crook's manager was ex-Newcastle United star Alan Shoulder and on shaking hands at the final whistle he said to me: "Tom, you will win this." I hoped he was right.

On returning to our dressing room - which was spartan at the very least - I found a buoyant group of players celebrating respectfully, with our opposition just a stud wall away. This was typical of my players who were largely mature family men. The younger players were all aware of my standards and principles and rubbing people's noses in it was a big no-no. I sought out my captain Terry Martin and winked at him saying: "Good decision that kicking into the wind first half" he smiled back at me and said: "We'll win this now".

I had a huge respect for Terry. He had been my skipper since our days at Sheppey. He held down a very important job at the Department of the Environment answering only to the minister who was at that time was Tory MP Michael Heseltine.

When Terry spoke I listened. He was the team's leader and spokesman. The players admired him because his level of performance never dropped. On the pitch he was my mouthpiece. The trust I had in him was unequivocal. The chairman popped his head around the door with a beaming smile on his face. He looked at me and mouthed the word "Wembley".

In the bar it was joyous. We had a number of supporters travel up from the south coast to watch the game. I was desperately trying to find out the other fourth round results. Journalist Mike Green said: "Leave it to me".

It was starting to feel serious. In the meantime amidst all the excitement, Roly was saying his goodbyes as Colin was getting ready to drive him home to see his wife and newborn son. I shook his hand as he got in my car and said: "Congratulations - don't be late for training Tuesday!" which he responded with a certain hand gesture! I went to the other side of the car shook Fordy's hand and thanked him.

We all went back into the hotel where the chairman had put a sizeable chunk of money behind the bar to allow his players to enjoy their evening without having to put their hands in their pockets.

FROM THE DEN TO WEMBLEY

Keith and I found a quiet corner and chatted about all things Wembley and were joined by journalist Mike Green who had the rest of the fourth round results.

Looking at them, I said to Keith: "Taunton are still in, so are Bedlington, Vauxhall Motors, Chippenham and us".

Keith looked at me and said: "It doesn't matter who we get we're good enough to beat anybody".

It was out of character for Keith to make such a bold statement. I admired him so much he had shared my journey for the last twelve years, but we were polar opposites. He was calm and considered, whereas I was emotional and volatile.

The rest of the players were sitting around the bar downing various beverages. I invited Jonny Warden over so we could all chat. Mike took the opportunity to interview our new signing.

Jon was 30 years old and listening to him proved to me I had signed the right guy. He was eloquent and, like Keith, very calm and considered.

I was 45 years of age and it dawned on the both of us that we had played against each other when I was at Bromley and he was at Kingstonian. I knew that he was going to add that something extra to our dressing room.

The following morning we left about eleven for the long trip home. Before I got on the coach I was watching the chairman pay our bill on his credit card so he could claim the air miles. Roy didn't miss a trick. Walking to the coach I thanked him for his generosity.

He turned and said to me "Tom, I'm happy to spend my cash, providing I get my money's worth, and you and your team have ticked that box many times over".

Roy was a great chairman. I always knew where I stood with him. I used to think I had the dream job here.

Climbing into bed that night I was exhausted and elated at the same time. In twelve short hours I would know our fifth round opponents, one game away from a place in the quarter finals.

The following lunchtime I listened to the draw via the FA's phone line. As each team was drawn out I ticked them off the list I had written. Deal Town's ball must have got stuck in the bag somewhere because when the penultimate ball was drawn we were still nowhere to be seen. That ball was the Metropolitan Police and then the voice said: "Will play Deal Town". I gave a big fist pump because we had beaten the Police earlier in the season at home in the FA Cup.

The Metropolitan Police played in a beautiful stadium in west London called Imber Court. Despite already having a report on the Police, I decided to watch them again, just because they had relaxed their rules about allowing non-serving policemen to play. This made it imperative to watch them so I went over on a Tuesday evening to watch them play, of all teams, Wembley.

Could that have been an omen for both sides?

That week, before our game, the rain had been incessant all over the country. Roy had again come up trumps for us booking a hotel right on Kingston Bridge for a light lunch at 12 noon.

With his permission I had invited the under 18s youth team just for the experience. One of my three central defenders, Marc Seager, had been running the youths since Peter Carman had left the club.

Seags was a very good left-footed central defender and he could throw the ball 30 yards. Because of the weather we had to ring to see if the pitch had been passed as playable. That done and the playing surface passed, we left Kingston to make the ten minute drive to Imber Court.

FROM THE DEN TO WEMBLEY

When we got there I had a huge decision to make about one of my midfield spots. I walked onto the pitch and as soon as I got there the surface was like a very soft pudding. My shoes sunk about an inch into the surface and I knew that the game was going to be a long 90 minute slog.

The pitch made my mind up who to play in midfield. Veteran Wayne Schweiso was my regular central midfielder for the last nine seasons and had just finished a 21-day suspension. He had played last Saturday in a cup match at Whitstable where I had played a less than full-strength side. I decided not to play Wayne purely because of his lack of game time in the previous weeks. This game was too important to make sentimental decisions about who should play or not. "Squeeze" was almost the first name on my teamsheet and had been for ten years. His replacement would be ex-Leyton Orient midfielder Barry Lakin. A super-talented player and great passer of the ball.

When I told Wayne he wasn't playing he was very angry, arguing the reasons behind my decision so much so he refused to come into the dressing room before the game. I told Colin and Keith what had happened. I hadn't consulted them before I had made my decision but they both agreed with me.

I had been mulling the problem over and over all week. Sometimes I did that, make a snap decision without consulting people. I always believed my gut instinct would stand me in good stead. On this occasion my gut instinct proved right as we ran out 5-2 winners. Steve Lovell won and buried a penalty early on. Roly made it two on 44 minutes and with Barry Lakin running the show, we scored three times in the last ten minutes.

After the game I learnt that Wayne had let his emotions run away with him and in his frustration had insulted the chairman and was gunning for me as well. I tried to placate him but eventually his mother and father, who followed their son everywhere, agreed to take him home. The whole situation left a bad taste in everyone's mouth.

The following day Roy rang me and said: "Tom, he has got to go." I asked him to let me talk to him but Roy was not budging: "No. It's unforgivable what he said to me."

I backed down: "OK, you're the boss, leave it to me".

Wayne was one of my best players and losing him at this particular time with us top of the league and in the quarter finals of the FA Vase could prove costly. Deep down I knew Roy was right. I wasn't party to Wayne's rant at Roy but what eye witnesses told me made me cringe. Later that evening I had to make one of the most difficult telephone calls of my short managerial career. When Wayne answered the phone I told him I'd had my orders to let him go. He growled at me down the phone muttering obscenities.

Despite this I still felt bad for him and promised to have another word with the chairman. To be fair to Wayne he apologised for letting me down, after all I had resurrected his football career when I signed him at Herne Bay nearly ten years previously.

After beating The Police I bumped into Steve Clarke who was the FA's competitions director, dealing with the Trophy, Vase and the FA Cup. He told me the sixth round draw was being held at 12:30 on Monday at Liverpool's Anfield ground.

He explained that if I wanted to go they would pay my expenses, including a hotel.

IF I wanted to go? I was there!

When I got home I immediately booked a hotel in Chester, a thirty minute drive to Liverpool. I was dealing with the Wayne Schweiso incident in the car whilst driving there. Eventually I had to pull into a motorway service area because it was all getting a bit much. I checked into my hotel and once settled I phoned Colin to talk to him about Wayne. He like me was really disappointed that we had lost such an important player.

Driving into Liverpool's ground the following morning I was like a little kid at Christmas. I had never been to Anfield so this was super exciting and I was ushered into the Bill Shankly suite where current Liverpool manager Gerard Houllier was to conduct the quarter final draw in about half an hour.

I sat down at a table and to my left was the manager of my Kent rivals Ramsgate Jim Ward. I had completely forgot that 'The "Rams' were also in the quarters. The Schweiso incident had made me lose my focus completely. It then suddenly dawned on me that an all Kent quarter final was a distinct possibility.

This was the day I met Chippenham manager Tommy Saunders. He was a large guy with an even larger personality. Jim and I got into a conversation with Tom. He was a lot younger than Jim and me but after ten minutes I warmed to him. He was loud and brash but very entertaining.

He had a view on all the other teams left in the quarters and wasn't afraid of letting everyone know.

Mr Houllier took his seat and with the trophy looming large on the table in front of him, proceeded to draw the numbers out of the pot in front of him.

Jim and I shook hands, saying good luck. We both knew our numbers. Deal Town were number two, Ramsgate four. Mr Houllier drew out the first number: "Two" he said, and for a moment time stood still.

I looked at Jim and raised my eyebrows. Could this really be an all Kent quarter final? Before Steve Clarke who was supervising the draw could say "Deal Town",

Houllier drew out number six and Steve said: "Will play Mossley".

I looked at Jim and we both shrugged our shoulders. Saunders whispered to me: "You are *both* lucky, you've missed us!" Ramsgate finally got an either or tie they would be playing the winners of Chasetown or Newcastle Town at home.

When it was all over I introduced myself to the Mossley contingent who were still scratching their heads wondering where the bloody hell Deal Town was. Mossley were members of the North Western Trains League along with Newcastle Town. I informed the Mossley chairman that Deal was eight miles along the coast from Dover, and recommended that as the best place if they were looking for a hotel, before wishing him all the best and saying my goodbyes. I turned to find Jim in an animated conversation with Mr Saunders.

Tommy's Chippenham had drawn the big favourites for the competition at home: Bedlington Terriers. Jim was disappointed with his either or draw because it meant he had to wait for a bit longer before he could start planning. Jim's captain Neil Brown had travelled up with him so as Jim would be a bit delayed before he left, I offered Neil a lift home to Herne Bay where we both now lived. Browny had been my captain when I was first took over at Herne Bay. We won the league that first season and Neil was a big influence in that dressing room.

Sadly that following season saw him and me part company due to his lack of game time. He duly went off to sign for Jim at Ramsgate. Me and Browny were by no stretch of the imagination mates, however I would like to think we had a healthy respect for one another.

Dropping Neil off at home I was still musing over the day's events. Mossley would mean more miles for Keith and me to drive to check up on our new opponents.

Keith, Colin and I chatted on the phone that night agreeing that whilst the tie looked tough on paper we all felt that being at home was vital.

At training the buzz from last Saturday's win at Crook was still tangible. The guys were peppering me with questions about Mossley.

During my research I discovered that an old apprentice colleague of mine had beaten me to Wembley.

George Duck was a second year apprentice when I joined Millwall in 1969. He left in 71 to join Southend from where he signed for Southern League club Wealdstone. George then left for Isthmian Premier League club Dagenham. He had scored over 250 goals for Wealdstone and ex-Stones manager Eddie Presland persuaded George to sign for The Daggers. This is where he scored his most famous goal at the end of that first season in 1979/80.

George found himself playing at Wembley for his new club against Northern League side, Mossley and he bagged the opening goal in a 2-1 win. He later joined Harrow Borough of the Isthmian League. Whilst there he continued to score freely.

I remember whilst playing for Bromley coming up against him in a couple of league encounters. His touch and hold-up play was still immaculate. His goalscoring touch was still at its sharpest but it didn't hurt playing for the best team in the league. He was held in the highest regard by everyone playing at that level.

His reputation as a stellar goalscorer preceded him everywhere he went. I was happy to tell everyone I knew: "Yeah, of course I know George Duck. We were mates at Millwall..." Name-dropping was one of my many talents!

I'd obtained Mossley's fixtures and decided I would go on my own to their next home fixture on a Tuesday night the following week, at home to Salford in a League Cup match. Keith said he would go up this Saturday coming and watch them play Maine Road in a league game.

Keith's report mirrored mine in many ways. Mossley had named the same team in both of the games we had watched, so it was important we knew what to expect. The week before we were due to play our quarter final, we were away to Erith Town in a league game where we had Marc Seager dismissed for handball on the goalline. Seags was a big player for us, he played in our back three and as I mentioned earlier he could throw the ball 30 yards.

The punishment for this game was an automatic one match ban. Luckily for all concerned we had a league game scheduled for Tuesday evening which meant Marc wouldn't miss the Mossley cup game. We were top of the league and a few wins away from being champions. Our opponents that Tuesday were struggling Lordswood, this meant I could give the majority of the first team a rest before Saturday's quarter final.

I had 22 players I could choose from, so with that in mind I promoted a couple of the youth team and a couple of the guys from the reserves who'd had plenty of Kent League games under their belts before I became first team manager.

A 3-0 win meant we were even closer to winning the league and it did wonders for Phil Turner's confidence, scoring twice.

There were four days to the biggest game in the club's history. Jim Ward's Ramsgate were playing their quarter final on the same day at home to Newcastle Town.

I spoke to Jim a couple of times that week. The local paper's sports editor Mark Stokes took Jim and I out for Lunch in Canterbury to write an article for that week's edition.

Because of our two local teams doing so well, their circulation figures had trebled. Everybody was dreaming of an all Kent Wembley final.

Our final training session before the quarter final was lighthearted and fun. The players' mood was excellent. I was always trying to think outside the box and Colin put it to the players that all of us wear women's underwear under their clothes this coming Saturday. Anybody ignoring this request would be fined. So at 2:15pm on the day of the game and with everyone in the dressing room I asked them to strip. The Mossley players had just arrived and I wondered what they would think of todays opposition if they were a fly on the wall in our dressing room.

There was an array of teddies and basques g-strings, stockings and suspenders on show. Everyone had taken part in the exercise, so no fines!

I was only a little concerned because one or two of the guys looked like they were enjoying themselves a little too much If only I had remembered to take my camera.

It was now 2:30pm and it was down to the serious business of trying to win a place in the semi final of the Vase. We recapped everything we had spoken about last Thursday.

The two sides walked out side by side in front of an estimated attendance of just under 1,000 people. Mossley had a sprinkling of supporters with flags hung over the railings behind the goal. It was a mild early spring day with watery sunshine. The pitch was in decent nick but was very hard underfoot.

We kicked off and after the first few minutes it was looking like the hard pitch might play a big part in the result. I was barking out orders to play the ball forward. After about three minutes, from a long goal-kick, a misguided header by the visitors' centre-half fell to our midfielder Jamie Kempster whose quick feet saw him flick the ball past the on-rushing 'keeper. I was thinking with my pragmatic head on. We had an invaluable early lead and it was vital that we continued to do the right things.

After about twelve minutes, an error by the Mossley centre half let Steve Lovell in but quick thinking from the Mossley 'keeper prevented him getting his shot away.

Within a couple of minutes Mossley's custodian pulled off a miraculous save from a Roly Graham strike from 18 yards. We could have been three goals to the good and it wasn't a quarter past three yet.

The hard surface was starting to dictate the game for both teams. I didn't want my players to get ahead of themselves, so again I got the message out to my captain, the ever reliable Terry Martin. That message was to get the ball forward to Steve Lovell's feet. Steve was 39 years old and taking a buffeting from the very physical Mossley defence.

As we approached half time Mossley got a goal from a corner, but the referee cut their celebrations short by ruling it out for a foul on our 'keeper Craig Tucker. I swallowed deeply, 1-1 at half time would have been an injustice, so the 1-0 lead we took into the dressing room was huge.

I asked Steve Lovell how was he feeling and if he wanted to come off. He looked me straight in the eye said to me firmly: "I don't want to fucking come off, I'm fine!". It wasn't a sentimental decision to leave him on. I was happy with his angry retort. He had been what I call a proper player and knew what his body could do. Every now and again I thought about Jim and what Ramsgate were doing.

15 minutes into the second half we won a corner which they cleared to their best and quickest player and having left ourselves short at the back, Terry Martin, who had

gone forward, was struggling to get back and win the ball from him. Ten yards from our penalty area and with my 'keeper rushing out to stop him scoring, Terry finally got his tackle in sending our visitor to the ground in an untidy heap.

There was a collective hush around the ground. Had Terry won the ball fairly or was it a professional foul? The referee waved play on and Craig cleared the loose ball out of the ground. Almost every Mossley player surrounded the referee, arguing that it was a foul and therefore a red card for Terry. I sat back and thought: "That looks a touch." I was too far away to judge correctly if Terry had fouled the lad or not.

The relief in seeing us still in the lead and keeping eleven men on the pitch was tangible. There were 25 minutes left as the game restarted with a Mossley throw in. Within seconds Jamie Kempster snapped into a tackle in our opponents' half, the ball falling to Steve Marshall, Lovell's strike partner. He pushed the ball past one hapless defender. Marshall had electric pace and, running at the heart of our visitors' defence, he dropped his shoulder once and, cutting back on his right foot, lashed a 20 yarder into the bottom corner of the Mossley net. All of us watching from the bench jumped up and punched the air.

There were 27 minutes left, I turned to Jon Warden and told him to get warmed up to go on for Steve. All I said to Jon was to go and impose himself on the two centre-halves. Keith put the number nine board up and. Steve shook hands with Jon and sat on the bench next to me as I congratulated him on his contribution to the day.

Minutes after Warden entered the fray he received a throw-in with his back to goal and, rolling his opponent on the byline, pulled it back for Jamie Kempster to strike from twelve yards. On this occasion the 'keeper parried the ball back into the penalty area straight to my right wing-back Paul Ribbens who gleefully smashed it back past the visitors' 'keeper to make it 3-0 with four minutes to go.

Mossley then had a player dismissed for dissent, yet remarkably managed to pull one back with a minute to go.

When the final whistle went I danced across the pitch to fall into the arms of my chairman. In the dressing room I raged about the goal we had given away late on. Unbeknown to me there had been some fisticuffs outside the dressing room at the end of the game. Meanwhile I tried to find out how Ramsgate got on.

I went into my office to phone Ramsgate's ground to see what was going on. For the next five minutes all I got was the engaged tone. I left it to someone else to tell me later. Everyone was ecstatic at our result. I was told by the secretary that Chippenham drew with Bedlington, and Vauxhall Motors had put five past Taunton. So all in all it had been a good day.

I walked back into the dressing room and, looking straight at Terry Martin, said with a huge grin: "Great tackle son!"

The draw for the semi finals was due to take place on Monday night at Fulham's Craven Cottage. I tried in vain to reach Jim and left the ground not knowing his result.

Whilst I was still at the ground I received a random call from an unknown number. I answered thinking it maybe someone wanting to congratulate me on today's result. It wasn't that at all. The voice at the other end of the line said in a broad Mancunian accent: "Is that Tommy Sampson, the manager of Deal Town?"

"Yes, that's right" I replied curiously.

"We've got your wife. We kidnapped her after the game" came the reply.

I detected a tone of mischief in his voice.

"Keep her" I said, "I've got no money to pay a ransom!"

"Where are you? I will come and get her."

I could hear him in the background asking where they were. He came back to me saying they were in the Kings Head on the seafront. I said: "OK, I will be there in 5 minutes".

I ran to the dressing room where a lot of the boys were now changed. I picked Jon Warden out and said to him: "Can you come with me, some Mossley fans have got Sandie in the Kings Head pub".

The Kings Head was owned by Graham Styles, one of the club's many sponsors. Pulling up outside the pub, Jon and I walked in to see Sandie sitting on a bar stool with a drink in her hand and her smile told me that this was a harmless stunt. Sandie explained she had been watching the game when it all kicked off. When a couple of guys stepped in to protect her, one asked her who she was here with. Sandie told him she was with the Deal manager. He then apologised to her for the Mossley supporters who were to blame for starting the scuffle. When the final whistle went, the Mossley guys who had protected Sandie playfully suggested they kidnap the manager's wife. Sandie, not feeling threatened, went along with the ruse.

When walking into Graham's pub I got a rousing welcome from the Mossley contingent. They were great lads and their congratulations for my team winning were sincere. They were mortified at the behaviour of their fellow fans. So once it had cost me £40 to buy them all a drink, Sandie, Jon and I drove back to the ground where, in the bar, the celebrations were still going on. It was a wonderful feeling to be at the helm of this ship. I was so proud of my players and my part in this wonderful journey. The chairman told me he would call me the next day with the details for going to Craven cottage on Monday for the semi-final draw. I had totally forgotten about how Ramsgate got on.

That night I couldn't help but think about that first day of pre-season at Sheppey when only eight players turned up, and here I was: "King of the Hill". I finally got the word that Jim's Ramsgate had lost 0-1 in extra time, so the last four were Chippenham or Bedlington, Newcastle Town, Deal Town and Vauxhall Motors. The favourites were Bedlington, Vauxhall Motors and Tommy Saunders's Chippenham.

It was difficult to get my head around being in the semi- finals. I had been dreaming of Wembley since my first day as a manager.

On the Monday our contingent from Deal met at the FA HQ in Soho Square our party included our fixture secretary and treasurer, chairman, Colin and me, as well as Dave Dadd the ex-manager.

We were all bussed to Fulham's Craven Cottage. When we got there we made our way to the suite where the draw was to be made by two ex-England legends Peter Shilton and World Cup-winning right-back George Cohen. We all sat down as Competitions Director Steve Clarke introduced the main protagonists. Every club in the last four were represented. We all knew our numbers because there was a chart with them front and centre. I sat next to the chairman. I had no pre conceived ideas as to who I wanted to play. The semi-final was over two legs, so for me it was my preference to be away from home first, I always thought it was better to be at home in the second leg, knowing what you had to do.

After the preliminaries were over, Cohen and Shilton started drawing the numbers out. First one out was Ramsgate's conquerors Newcastle Town, followed by Deal Town's number. So that was our fate. If we were to get to Wembley, the final part of this journey was to start in Staffordshire.

I found Newcastle's assistant manager and player manager over the buffet. Manager Ray Walker was a really nice guy whereas his number two Martin Smith was a miserable surly individual. He let slip that they would be coming to watch us very soon. I assured him that we'd be watching them too.

Our next game was away to our nearest challengers in the league, Thamesmead Town, where I reshuffled my pack. The players that needed a break were Steve Lovell and Roly Graham.

I had two players who could throw the ball 30 yards. Marc Seager and Paul Ribbens. I told both of them under no circumstances throw the ball long tonight, believing that Smith and Walker from Newcastle would be watching. Why give them all of the information about us on a plate.?

The two legs would both be played on a Sunday. This was because Newcastle Town's ground was less than 200 yards from Stoke City's and because Stoke were due to meet Manchester United, the police decided they didn't want to handle the both games on the same day.

The Vase committee instructed Newcastle to travel to Deal the following Sunday for the second leg. Our first leg was three weeks away. As usual my secretary gave me a list of Newcastle's fixtures. Keith and I decided to watch them play as soon as possible.

Our first opportunity was the coming Saturday where our opponents were away to Atherton Collieries. Atherton was just outside Manchester near Wigan. Keith and I set off early that Saturday morning leaving Colin to oversee the first team's Kent Senior Trophy semi-final against County League side Bearsted. Keith and I pulled into a motorway services for a proper meal before we carried on to Manchester.

En route we decided to visit Newcastle's ground to suss out the facilities. We parked and sneaked up the slope at the back of one terrace. The pitch was surrounded by a tarmac cycling track. Down below us we watched intently as their players were filing on to a coach. We felt like a couple of spies from a James Bond film! We got back in the car and drove out of the stadium. Stoke City's ground momentarily appeared in the distance to our left and we picked up the motorway towards Manchester and an hour later we pulled into the home of Atherton Collieries.

There were no programmes, only sheets of paper with the teams printed on. We walked into the bar and ordered our drinks then wandered outside. There was no seating area, just ramshackle terraces I looked at Keith and said to him: "What a dump!"

We found our way to the back of the main terrace and at 2:45 Keith and I were the only two people in the ground on a beautiful sunny March day. The teams jogged out from the dressing room in an eerie silence.

The game kicked off and I turned to Keith and said "Something's not right here".

I couldn't believe what I was seeing, especially when I noticed the linesman running the line was wearing jeans and normal shoes, a jumper and shirt and tie.

Keith said: "I'm going to have a wander and see what I can find out".

When he came back he was grinning from ear to ear. He looked at me and said: "Tom, we're watching a reserve game" I looked back at him: "You're fucking joking!"

Atherton were playing Newcastle away and we were watching their reserve teams.

It dawned on me he was right. It was 3:25 so feeling the worst sense of embarrassment, I said: "Let's go, we'll get back to Newcastle and catch the second half".

That was a bit optimistic. We pulled into the ground

with about ten minutes to go and, finding a place on the terraces, we watched Atherton score a late penalty.

When the final whistle went we followed everybody into the bar and after a little while joined in a conversation with some local supporters. We admitted we were from Deal on scouting duties.

Over the next ten minutes we pumped them for information about their team for next Sunday. We learned that so and so was suspended and someone else was injured. Keith and I never let on we had only seen the last five minutes. Eventually Newcastle's player manager walked into the bar and all the guys we had been talking to couldn't wait to draw his attention to the fact that two Deal Town spies were in the bar.

I shook Ray's hand and introduced him to Keith. Ray then offered to show me the dressing rooms. They were adequate, no more.

When Keith and I got in the car we looked at each other. I said to Keith: "No-one must find out about today!" We are now a secret society of two!

I told him I would speak to Ramsgate's manager Jim Ward for as much information as I could get. Keith and I still felt really embarrassed by the days events. I said to him:: "If we win the Vase we'll confess!"

As I said it my phone rang. It was the chairman. "How did it go?: He asked.

I told him they had been beaten 0-1 with a late penalty. We had won 1-0 which meant we were in the final of the Kent Senior Trophy. Games were coming thick and fast. A two leg FA Vase semi-final and a Kent Senior Trophy final - as well as league games.

We had two training nights to prepare for the Vase first leg next Sunday. Where the games were concerned I wasn't too bothered. I had built a squad of 22 players which I felt was enough to deal with the workload. I spoke at length to Jim that week. I knew it was difficult for him talking about the team that had ended his dream of Wembley. The best information I got that week was from those Newcastle fans in their bar. We were going to travel up on Saturday and stay in a hotel just outside Stoke.

When we got to our hotel it was on a trading estate. In the corner, next to our hotel, was a bowling alley. I heard mumblings of excitement about it. As we parked I got to the door and said at the top of my voice "Don't even think about it!"

I had given every player a strict itinerary. For the weekend. Whilst relaxing in the hotel reception I could hear a bit of a commotion coming from the bar. I looked at Colin and asked him to go and find out what it was all about.

He came back a few seconds later saying: "You're not going to like this" I looked at him quizzically.

"Monty and Ribbo have been bowling."

David Monteith and Paul Ribbens were my wing-backs and very important in the system we played. I asked Colin to send them in to see me. I was furious that these two players had blatantly disobeyed my instructions. They both approached me somewhat sheepishly.

"You want to see us boss?" Monty said nervously. I nodded.

"Is it true you both went bowling?"

"Yep we did" came the reply.

"Did you not hear me when we drove in? I said: don't even think about going bowling"

Ribbo piped up: "Sorry Boss. we never heard you say that"

I was having none of it: "It says on your itinerary, no-one leaves the hotel under any circumstances. Don't you two realise that tomorrow you are playing the biggest game in your life? You are both 180 minutes from playing at Wembley stadium."

I was so angry that ,without taking a second to evaluate what these young lads had done, I angrily said: "Right, that's it, you are both on a train home in the morning".

Keith shouted at me: "Whoa! Tom, think about it."

Calming suddenly, I said I would make my mind up later that night.

Keith and I chatted about it for a further 15 minutes. I was so disappointed in what these boys had done. I decided to let them sweat for a couple of hours. Monty and Ribbo were vital to the way we played so sending them home would be like cutting your own nose off to spite your face.

Keith and I were on our third pot of tea when my captain Terry Martin came in asking for a quiet word about Monty and Ribbo. He said: "I've spoken to them and they genuinely did not hear you about the bowling."

I told Terry that I wasn't going to send them home but added: "Don't tell them that yet."

That was typical of Terry, fighting his players' corner. Colin came and sat down and I explained what I was going to do. He agreed it was the right decision. I had said on the players' itinerary that they should go to bed only when they were ready. Stipulating a time would be treating them like children.

As usual on occasions like this I was rooming with my great friend Colin. We were both still in the bar at gone eleven. Most of the guys had retired for the night. We only had one problem for tomorrow's game and that was Roly Graham's badly bruised foot, an injury sustained in the previous Tuesday evening's league match with Whitstable Town where two goals from Jon Warden sealed a 2-1 win. Unfortunately for Roly he picked up this foot injury. So Tomorrow he would need a fitness test before the game.

Roly's' importance to the team could not be underestimated. He had played for me at Herne Bay scoring bucketloads of goals he then followed me to Deal where his goalscoring feats made him a crowd favourite. He didn't have a particular role in the team, I let him roam freely, only asking him to muck in when he had to.

We were in the middle of March and he had already scored 18 goals. I was pretty sure Newcastle would have a plan in place for Roly so if he failed his fitness test and Phil Turner played instead it would throw a spanner in the works of Newcastle Town's planning.

As soon as we got to the ground Keith and Colin put Roly through his paces. Phil Turner knew if Roly failed to come through his test he would play in his place. Phil and I watched Roly's test intently, me hoping he would pass, Phil thinking the opposite.

Roly passed and proved his right to play. I consoled Phil as much as I could. My pre-match team talk was a bit Churchillian. My theme was to play the game and not the occasion. When I finished there was lots of noise and clapping, players embracing one another and good lucks being shouted.

The buzzer went and out of the dressing room door went the players led by Terry. I shook Colin's hand and said "Good luck" Keith and I embraced one another knowing that this was the culmination of nearly of nearly two decades hard work and we made our way to the dugouts.

The game kicked off and after the first few minutes of sizing one another up, we won a throw-in over the far side. Paul Ribbens then threw the ball 30 yards into the Newcastle six yard box, where in a vain attempt to clear, the Newcastle centre forward who was back defending headed the ball into his own goal. Not allowing Ribbo to take a long throw at Thamesmead a week ago had paid off as Newcastle didn't know how to handle it.

As part of the celebrations Dave Monteith ran right in front of Colin and I mimicking bowling a ball down the alley.

"Fuck you, you little bastard!" I shouted at him. I wanted the final whistle to blow there and then. We all sat down and chatted amongst the three of us. " What a start!" Colin "said.

I was on my feet barking orders and for the rest of the first half we took control of the game. In the 32nd minute we won another throw-in on the far side in an identical position, so up stepped Ribbo.

This time he didn't throw it so far and as we had rehearsed many times, Steve Lovell found a little pocket of space on the angle of the six yard box where he flicked the ball on to the penalty spot and it bounced up kindly for my onrushing central midfielder Steve Best to head past a bemused Newcastle 'keeper.

I couldn't believe just what had happened. Deep into the first half here we were two goals to the good in the FA Vase semi-final

Again I was on my feet, screaming at Terry Martin to keep it tight until half time. We turned the screw, penning Newcastle back, their body language became increasingly negative. I was constantly looking at my watch, counting the seconds to half time. This road to Wembley was going to take its toll on me. I'd had my wife kidnapped and yesterday's bowling gate drama.

The half time whistle went and I turned towards the dressing room. Opening the door the players followed me in with me thinking about the importance of saying the right things.

"Don't pat yourselves on the back just yet." I began.

"We have to regroup and start all over again".

I pointed at the wall separating the two dressing rooms. "What you've got in there is a wounded animal. The next thing to do is kill it off. "

I looked at Terry and said: "You're the captain of this team, so it's your job to see we do the right things". The second half started and their player manager Ray Walker had brought himself on. Ray had played many times for Port Vale and was considered the best midfielder outside the Premier League.

To be fair to the hosts they had a real go. We weren't sitting back, we were being penned back. Terry was his usual unflappable self and Steve Lovell was doing his best to hold it up for us as the game crept into its final minutes. Both Roly and Steve Marshall were denied goals by last-ditch defending and great goalkeeping until eventually the final whistle sounded.

There were no elaborate celebrations, which was great we didn't want to antagonise our opponents unduly. In seven days we had to do it all over again. I was so proud of my players and Keith and Colin as well.

The mood in the dressing room was joyous. I did ask the players to keep the noise down as the opponents dressing room was so close. The last thing I wanted was to give the Newcastle dressing room any extra motivation for next week's return.

The chairman had laid on a coach for all the friends and family to come and see the game. In a moment of quiet I thanked the players for their commitment and courage not just for today, but in previous times. Terry Martin had won the Carlsberg Man of the Match award so he was called outside for the presentation and press photographs.

When he returned everyone was ready to go and see their friends and relatives in the bar. Roy had been so generous during our Vase run laying on luxury coaches and where the players were concerned nothing was too much trouble, a truly great man. We weren't going back to the hotel, we were going straight home. You could feel the joy on the coach as we left The Potteries.

About half an hour into our journey my phone rang. It was Ramsgate's Jim Ward asking how it had gone. When I calmly told him we had won 2-0 I detected a sharp intake of breath before he said: "Fantastic congratulations".

The coming week was going to be hectic. I was going to be in the office every day selling tickets for next Sunday's second leg which was going to be all-ticket and probably the toughest day of my football career to date.

Here we were holding a two goal advantage from the first leg and along with that unbeaten at home for almost 18 months. Newcastle couldn't come and beat us 3-0. Surely not. Or could they?

When we got back I offered Jonny Warden a lift home as we both lived in Herne Bay. I pulled into a petrol station on the way home to fill up with fuel, when I went to pay the guy behind the till he took my money and said: "Congratulations Mr Sampson!"

Thanking him, this was the first time I realised what an impact we were having on the community. I thought back to those early days when I first arrived and the depth of bad feeling there was towards me and my team. We had turned that animosity on its head and now we were all heroes.

The next week was so busy with people queuing up to purchase tickets. Roy's wife Billie was helping as was Annette Bryant, Roy's personal assistant. The stream of people coming through the office seemed endless! Roy had 2.500 tickets printed and, realising the demand also arranged for two 500 seater temporary stands to be erected on the far side of the ground. It was Tuesday and the stands were due to be in place by Friday afternoon.

Still the steady stream of people came and as each person saw me they would ask me: "When will the tickets for Wembley be on sale?"

I tried to play it down saying "It's not over yet", but it was hard to hide my own excitement and anticipation of how close we were now.

Our pitch was OK but in an attempt to make it more suitable for the occasion Roy pulled a few strings and managed to get the greenkeeping staff from Royal St George's Golf Course to come and tend to it.

So, on the Thursday and Friday before the big game the ground was a hive of activity. The staff from St George's were hard at it as well as the company erecting the temporary stands. The Police also visited to advise us on Health and Safety. Fortunately for us, Dover Athletics stewards had agreed to come and help us on the day.

All the time this was happening the Deal public were purchasing tickets. The Police set a ground capacity of 2000. Roy also had a marquee being erected for the various club officials and dignitaries attending the game. Our shirt sponsors were a Skoda dealership in the town. They gave us £5000 towards our expenses for the day. I estimated that the chairman paid at least £20,000 out of his own pocket to put the day on.

I had been in the ground all week and my brain was working overtime on the details for Sunday. Roy could see how tired I was and he very kindly said to me: "Tom, go home and have a break". I thanked him for the offer but before going to my car I walked across the pitch, climbed to the top of one of the temporary stands and once there I looked all around. What a fantastic view supporters were going to have of the game. I let my mind wander and thought about my late mum Maisie and my late wife Carole and how proud they would have been of me. I sat back and cast my eye around the ground, it looked an absolute picture. I not ashamed to admit that I felt very emotional and shed a little tear.

I was now 46 years of age and within 90 minutes of fulfilling a boyhood dream. I turned the key in the ignition of my car and drove out of the ground almost in a dream. I had agreed with the players we would have a light training session on Saturday lunch time and after around 30 minutes we all got showered and changed and made our way into the clubhouse. Everybody was told: no alcohol only soft drinks.

We sat around chatting about the next day and I reminded them be in the dressing room for 2pm sharp.

The local television station ITV Meridian were going to cover the game live. We all then went our separate ways. Driving home all sorts of doubts entered my head. What happens if they score first? I had always been something of a pessimist during my career, that way the pain of disappointment isn't so bad.

My exterior self was full of confidence to the point of arrogance. I hated to show any type of weakness. To my players I was their leader almost to the point where I could wear my underpants outside my trousers!

The local school had offered to open up its car park to allow the players and their friends to park, as it was going to be extremely busy in the local side streets.

As I pulled into the school car park Jon Warden also pulled in. We both got out of our cars, and after locking up we strolled across the road and into the ground.

Jon was a calm laid back individual and our conversation albeit short was around the prospect of getting to Wembley. We both knew that in less than two hours time we could be on our way to the holy grail of English football, Wembley Stadium!

FROM THE DEN TO WEMBLEY

Getting into the dressing room I took the team sheet out of my briefcase and pinned it up on the notice board. Jon read it over my shoulder and saw his name alongside the number twelve. He understood his role in the team. It was purely to replace Steve Lovell after about 70 minutes. Knowing Jon was ready to replace him late in the game meant Steve was free to run himself into the ground for us. He was great at holding the ball up but his days of running the channels were long gone. I held him in the highest regard.

As much as I craved Wembley I wanted it for Steve as well. Retirement was growing ever closer for him. I thought if I could give him one last day in the spotlight, what a wonderful way for him to ride off into the sunset with Wembley on his already impressive CV.

Steve and I had a very professional relationship I would always take on board his opinion and he was happy to allow me to get on with managing my team. We would play the occasional round of golf together and it was during these that we discussed the team and the system we played.

I knew he wasn't that keen on the 3-5-2 formation I preferred. I valued his opinion but I was a very strong-minded person and it would take an awful lot of persuasion to get me to budge. I was very much a "second place is first place for losers" type of guy.

I was driven to the point of obsession. I would analyse every detail before I was satisfied I could move on. The players started to arrive and I looked at everyone for a clue to their mindset. I always insisted they read the teamsheet I had pinned up because I didn't want anyone taking their place in the side for granted, even my captain Terry Martin.

At approximately 2:30pm I started to go through all of the details regarding our dead ball kicks, tactics and the like.

Everybody was in good spirits with little evidence of nerves despite this being the biggest game of their lives. We were 2-0 up from the first leg and it was imperative we did not sit back. So, bang on three o'clock the buzzer went off to signal for us to leave the dressing room. The Stadium was humming, the two temporary stands were both packed and everywhere you looked it was four deep.

When the game kicked off the skies were very threatening. I reached into my blazer pocket to look at the photograph of my late mum and wife. Purely because I felt comforted by it. To my dismay it wasn't there and I realised that I had left it in my briefcase in the dressing room.

I asked one of my subs could they could go to the dressing room and get it for me. I gave Ricky Bennett the combination to my briefcase where he could pick up the envelope the photo was in and bring it back to me. After about 15 minutes Ricky hadn't returned. I hadn't been paying a lot of attention to the game and then suddenly Rick appeared. He gave me the envelope which I opened and looked at my treasured photograph and precisely at that moment the crowd roared as Roly scored to give us a 3-0 aggregate lead. I actually missed the goal because I was looking at the photo.

Jonny Warden put his arm around me and said: "This has got your name all over it".

I didn't understand his reasoning for that statement until I got home later that afternoon and I saw on the local news how fortuitous Roly's goal had been, rebounding off of his knee from about 20 yards.

I couldn't believe that the moment I looked at my photo we scored. The bench leapt up to celebrate the goal. So, in an instant I jumped as well. Keith and I embraced. The three subs and Colin were drunk with ecstasy.

Just a quarter of an hour after we'd kicked off we were suddenly three goals clear and within touching distance of Wembley. We saw the first half out 1-0.

As the players settled down in the dressing room I said: "Let's go back a week, we are in that boat again, we have a clear lead, the only thing that can beat us now is ourselves".

The buzzer went again and the players filed out the door. I pulled Terry Martin back and said: "It's up to you now, you are my captain, you must lead from the front. Don't let us lose our tempo. We have to play to our strengths now"

He looked me square in the eye and said: "Don't worry Tom, we'll get there". I had so much respect for Terry. He had been my captain for ten years now, he had an exceptional temperament, never flustered, never indecisive and led by example.

I followed him out of the door, walking across the pitch in front of the old terrace which was packed with probably 1200 fans. The reception Terry and I received sent shivers down my spine. He was so focussed he didn't even acknowledge them while I waved and clapped them back. Terry was a cool customer with ice in his veins, he took his responsibilities as captain very seriously and nothing was going to distract him.

As the second half progressed those threatening dark clouds that we started with opened up, sending a torrent of rain down, quickening up the pitch which suited us and allowed my two wing-backs to threaten them down the flanks. Ribbens and Monteith, my two bowling pals, were relentless. Their contribution to my team was one of our greatest strengths, their stamina levels were incredible. We were now in the last 20 minutes of the most important game I had ever been involved in.

I told Jonny Warden to warm up as I would be putting him on for Steve Lovell. The two teams had cancelled each other out since half time. Our visitors were very reluctant to throw people forward which I found strange.

Steve came off and Jon duly took his place up front. The Newcastle players seemed resigned to their fate and had lost the will to fight. Then suddenly a long overhit cross was met by our opponents striker who headed it across our goaline where it was blasted into our net by one of Newcastle's midfielders from about three feet making it 3-1 to us with just nine minutes to go.

As the away goal didn't apply to this game, Newcastle would have to score three more goals in those final moments to win the tie. I can't lie to you, those last few minutes seemed to take an age, when in truth, our opponents were gone.

We dominated the ball in those closing stages and Newcastle gave in to the inevitable. The final whistle blew and almost like they'd been shot, every Newcastle player slumped to the ground. Steve Lovell threw his arms around my neck shouting: "You've done it, YOU'VE DONE IT!'"

Steve and I walked onto the pitch which had been invaded by hundreds of supporters. People were patting me on the back and singing "We're going to Wembley..."

I was dragged away to speak to the local radio station. By this time I was sobbing with joy.

My next task was to find Keith and Colin, before making it to the door of our dressing room which I opened to witness sheer joy. The champagne corks were popping - courtesy of the chairman. Before I could join in the celebrations I was dragged off to speak to Meridian Television which for me was not a chore.

Bizarrely the sun had replaced the pouring rain and I conducted my television interview in bright light. It still hadn't dawned on me the size of what we had achieved this afternoon. I was going to take my team to Wembley!

FROM THE DEN TO WEMBLEY

Me celebrating our quarter final victory over Mossley FC with Deal Town charman Roy Smith.

My late wife Carole (left) and late mum Maisie - the treasured photo I was looking at when Roly scored the goal that clinched our place at Wembley

FROM THE DEN TO WEMBLEY

Me with Jim Ward (Ramsgate Manager) discussing our quarter final matches

Marc Seager - Central defender wins another aerial battle, also my youth team manager

Making my way back across the pitch to the dressing room I stumbled on my chairman. He gave me a radio microphone and told me to address the fans of which there was several hundred still on the pitch. I can't remember what I said because of the noise. I know I thanked everyone including Roy and the players. Roy then whispered to me the official attendance was 2495. I was so proud of myself and the players.

We would be meeting Western League side Chippenham Town at Wembley on May 6th 2000. Today was 26th March which meant we had 7 weeks to prepare.

I phoned Tommy Saunders the Chippenham Boss and congratulated him on his team's success. The build up to Wembley was going to be fun, simply because we could both be outrageous at times. We were both confident characters. If not a little arrogant. The outspoken nature of our characters meant that in the build up there wasn't going to be a dull moment.

After addressing the fans I found my way to the special marquee that Roy had put up. There were over 150 people in the tent from Kent and Staffordshire. I received plaudits from both sides of that day's football divide, it was fantastic to see players with their mums and dads, wives, brothers sons, and daughters.

I'll never forget Terry Martin's father giving me an emotional bear hug and seeing his mum in tears because she was going to see her son lead Deal Town out of the Wembley tunnel beneath those iconic Twin Towers.

I gradually worked the room enjoying the occasion. I was at pains to let people know that this wasn't all down to me, highlighting Keith's and Colin's contributions.

The local press outlets were working feverishly talking to players, getting their stories. Terry and I found a quiet corner to reminisce about the last decade or so from Sheppey United to Herne Bay and now Deal Town. My last port of call was Steve Lovell. We had seven weeks until Wembley and eleven league games left to play as well as a Kent Senior Trophy final. I told him: "Don't expect to play every week".

He looked at me with that steely glare of his and said: "Tom I have to play to keep fit"

"Yes" I answered, "but not every game!"

He shrugged his shoulders and said he'd leave it up to me. I had two players trying to shake off injuries, defender Jason Ash who, despite a slight thigh problem, had played in both semi-final legs. He'd had the injury since the turn of the year and had to pass fitness tests for both legs, so he was another player I told wouldn't play every game between now and Wembley.

The other player was my photo-saving sub Ricky Bennett. I had given Rick a timeline to get fit and like Jason, had got himself fit enough to take his place on the bench today.

I was still very emotional. I think that was partly due to the size of the achievement as well as the stories that came out of our dressing room. For example, Steve Lovell was probably going to be playing his last ever game of an incredibly distinguished career at Wembley. He had already confided in me that he wouldn't be playing next season. It had been an honour and a privilege to have him play for me at my humble little club.

Also there was my left wing back David Monteith, who had signed for me at Sheppey United twelve years ago when he was seventeen. David was now 29 and on his journey to Wembley had suffered no less than three very serious ACL (anterior cruciate ligament) injuries. To watch him fight back and regain his football career was so inspirational. Monty was like the son I never had. I certainly loved him like one and had long since forgiven him for his part in the bowling gate fiasco!

I wasn't the only one feeling emotional. Jon Warden was close to shedding a tear. He said to me: "Tom, I know I am probably going to be on the bench at Wembley but I want to thank you for getting me so close". It was difficult to think about leaving this gathering.

My last conversation was with the chairman. Roy told me that negotiations with Dover District Council were not going well. His dream of redeveloping the stadium were foundering on the rocks.

I pulled away from the ground with adrenaline still pumping through my veins I stopped just before turning left into St Leonard's Road. I switched the radio on and heard myself being interviewed by my friend and guest at Crook Town, Mike Green.

I was a little embarrassed at hearing myself blubbing live on radio. I also spared a thought for Wayne Schweiso who had committed football career suicide at the Metropolitan Police game in the fifth round a few weeks back. I wondered what would be going through his mind sitting at home knowing the chance of playing at Wembley had passed him by.

I carried on with my journey home, the feeling of elation and ecstasy still burning bright. I had shaken hands with Newcastle's player manager Ray Walker before I left, offering my sympathy for his team losing. I didn't envy his trip home.

I got home and put my briefcase down, but not before I got out the match programme to read. I jumped in the shower and felt the stress of the day leave my body. I couldn't help thinking about that 15-year-old boy starting his first day as an apprentice back in 1969.

The experiences I had lived through since then fully justified all those decisions I had made since. Dropping out of the league to join Dartford then Welling and after that Bromley then Tooting & Mitcham, Erith

FROM THE DEN TO WEMBLEY

&Belvedere, Tonbridge Angels and on to Sheppey United, Herne Bay and finally here at Deal Town.

My phone was red hot that night people offering their congratulations and, of course, cheekily asking about tickets for Wembley!

During those seven weeks that I had to prepare, I was in a quandary as to whether or not to rest players. We were battling with Thamesmead Town at the top of the table.

The Tuesday night after the second leg we were due to play Sheppey United who were ground sharing with Sittingbourne.

In the previous 24 hours I had signed a prolific goalscorer, the ex-Margate, Welling United and St Johnstone, striker Martin 'Bugsy' Buglione. Bugsy and I were old friends. During a short spell as player manager at Tonbridge Angels in the mid-80s I signed him as a raw 17-year-old from Conference League team Welling United.

I picked him to play in the Sheppey game and typically he opened the scoring in a 4-0 rout. Steve Marshall added two more quickly with long throw specialist Paul Ribbens scoring late on.

I now had a squad of 22 players and with still five weeks to go before Wembley everything was looking rosy. Because of the size of the Chippenham game, we had to make several trips to Wembley to get advice about ticketing and marketing.

Roy's assistant Annette Bryant took responsibility for ticket sales. I was given the task of organising hotel accommodation. I knew Chippenham were going to stay in Kensington, whereas I wanted to be a bit further out.

I contacted The Burnham Beeches hotel near Windsor. The hotel is where the England squad stayed for the 1996

Euros. I gave them numbers and relevant information and on receiving their quote for a 48 hour stay, I ran it past Roy and got the thumbs up. The game couldn't come soon enough now.

Roy had British Telecom install a designated Wembley phone line so that people could order their tickets. As with the semi final second leg, people queued around the ground to purchase their precious tickets. I had been in the non-league world for the last 26 years and had never experienced anything like this.

Several of the players were being followed by Meridian Television cameras. For those guys it only highlighted how big the game was. The league championship was sewn up three weeks before Wembley with a home victory over our main rivals Thamesmead Town. A 2-0 win saw us win the league by a nine point margin with the usual suspects on the scoresheet: Roly Graham and Steve Marshall.

I was in the ground early the day after the second leg. I had to confirm Burnham Beeches as well as listing who was rooming with who.

As each day passed it got more and more hectic with both radio and television interest. Roy was still battling with Dover District Council. The main stumbling block was the council wanted to take possession of the new facility when the lease ran out.

Roy wanted it to be the club's responsibility. Roy's legal team were encouraging him to stand his ground, after all it was his money he was spending. The facility would help Deal Town to be self sufficient in the future.

In the meantime it was my responsibility to organise getting suits made for the players to wear at Wembley. I got in touch with all of the main clothing outlets. Marks & Spencers Next and Burtons. I went to visit all of the senior management people to plead my case.

The people at Next in the Bluewater Shopping Centre near Dartford came to my rescue saying if we could choose off the peg suits they would do 15% discount. Their management team offered to open early one Saturday morning to get the players to come in and choose their shirts and suits and I agreed this.

All that was left was for me to organise the players. I arranged for the guys to meet at Bluewater early one Saturday morning where Next would open especially for us.

The players looked at and tried on the suits and any alterations were noted. About two hours later we had to leave for Next to open their doors to the public.

We all left for home about 9:30am some players were happy to take their gear with them. Those who needed alterations done left me with the task of picking their suits up later in the week. The suits were paid for out of a substantial sponsorship by a care home company called Robinia. The only stipulation they required from us was that wherever the players wore the suits they would wear a Robinia emblem on their breast pocket. As these suits wouldn't be worn before Wembley the small cloth emblem could be loosely attached the night before the big day.

I had been a non-league football manager for 19 years now and this was a whole new kettle of fish!

The buzz about Wembley was intoxicating. On my way home from the ground one day I stopped off at a Little Chef to get some lunch where halfway through my meal, out of the corner of my eye, I spotted an elderly gentleman making his way towards me. As he got to my table he reached out his hand and said:

"Tom, sorry to bother you but I have been supporting Deal Town for 55 years and I just wanted to thank you for everything you have done for the club since you have been here".

I shook his out stretched hand. I felt very humble. Here was a man I'd never met and I have somehow touched his life. I considered myself very fortunate to be in the position I had found myself in.

During the weeks leading up to Wembley we still trained on a regular basis. It was vital that we got to Wembley with fitness levels intact. We beat Faversham Town over two legs to reach the League Cup Final. That League Cup final was scheduled for Saturday 6th May the same day as the Vase final!

The Kent League management committee in their flawed wisdom decided to bring it forward one week to the 29th April. When I heard, I went straight to the chairman protesting: "There is no way I am risking my players one week before Wembley".

He agreed with me and said we would go back to the Kent League and seek another date.

We were due to play VCD Athletic. The Kent League refused to budge. I phoned everyone on the management committee to plead our case but I came up against a wall of intransigence.

The chairman was as exasperated as me and suggested we send the youth team. I wasn't having that.

"No way! I don't want it in the record books that the same year the club went to Wembley they lost in the League Cup final to VCD Athletic!".

I suggested to the Kent League that they put it back a week and gamble on Deal winning the FA Vase. Because if we did there would be 3,000 people at the game rather than a three-figure crowd. I thought that made perfect sense but again the answer was an emphatic "No", so we took the tough decision to concede the game to our opponents. Faversham, who we beat in the semi-final, were promoted to play in the final where they lost 1-4 in front of 150 people!

Two weeks before Wembley we were due to play Chatham Town in the final of the Kent Senior Trophy at Sittingbourne's vast Central Park Stadium.

Once again I put it to the players if were happy playing. Everybody said yes despite knowing that a minor injury could see them miss out on the greatest day of their footballing lives. I was pretty sure that Chippenham's Tommy Saunders would probably be there having one last look at us before Wembley.

With that in mind, on the day I promoted three youth team players and left out regulars Jason Ash, Steve Lovell and goalkeeper Craig Tucker. Despite this we went on to pummel Chatham 5-1, Phil Turner scoring a brilliant hat-trick and Roly Graham getting his 101st goal since signing for me at Herne Bay in 1992.

Roly was an enigma in many ways. I had always given him free rein and he had rewarded me many times over. Keith and I had now won six trophies in our partnership together over ten years.

All those successes had my name on them but Keith's contribution was a major influence and should never be forgotten.

Finally the big day arrived.

We all decided to meet in Dartford on the Friday and drive in our own cars to our hotel. We did it this way so that players would be at liberty to leave when they wanted to on the Sunday following the game.

Our coach that Roy had booked especially for the players would be waiting for us at Burnham Beeches because we were going to Wembley on Friday afternoon for a tour of the stadium.

Chippenham were also going to be touring the stadium before us. One of my stalwart players Steve Forrest who had played for me since the Herne Bay days was expecting a call from his wife Emma because she was due to give birth at anytime, and as Sod's Law would have it, just as we all pulled into the hotel grounds his phone went off to say that Emma was in labour. Steve had no choice but to turn his car around and drive back home to Canterbury. Steve wasn't in the team for tomorrow's final because of an old knee injury, although he was going to be on the bench as a reward for his loyalty and service playing for me over the years.

This was not a sentimental decision, I just wanted him to walk out of that tunnel and sing the national anthem with all of his colleagues and manager. Steve was well aware that his chances of playing any part in the game were remote.

After booking in we all got changed into our Wembley tracksuits and filed onto the coach for our short trip to Wembley and our tour. As we pulled into the car park we passed the Chippenham coach going back to their hotel in Kensington.

Pulling up outside these two huge oak doors at the rear of the stadium, we alighted from our extremely luxurious coach where we were met by a very well dressed man in his Wembley blazer. I introduced myself as the manager and he gave me strict instructions as to where we could go and where we couldn't. The committee members' wives could not walk on the pitch in their heels!

We were actually at the base of the stadium's legendary tunnel. Both dressing rooms were located just inside on the left and right.

Our dressing room tomorrow would be on our right. This was the away dressing room. As we all entered it was hugely underwhelming. Ordinary iron pegs to hang your clothes on, and very old plaster-boarded walls.

The sense of history was palpable. Moore, Charlton, Banks, Hurst, Stiles, Ball, Ramsey, Hunt, Cohen, Wilson, Peters. I was old enough to remember that famous day in 1966 and for me it was very emotional.

After a short while our guide ushered us all back into the tunnel and encouraged everyone towards the pitch and the ladies present were asked to remove their shoes. When I walked out of that tunnel I was in the company of my captain Terry Martin and the very experienced Steve Lovell. I believe that the three of us all had to swallow deeply. I was taken aback by the size of the stadium. I had watched many cup finals on television and was amazed at how insignificant I felt. All of the players wandered towards the far goal or as I called it: 'Geoff Hurst's hat-trick goal'.

We all sat down on the goaline for photos to be taken. From there we all made for the Royal Box. I was eager to see where I would be sitting tomorrow. Keith and I chatted about where we had been and where we had come from. I am happy to admit that I shed a tear on his shoulder. I was thinking to myself: how was I going to handle tomorrow?

There were many photos taken that afternoon. I was quietly confident having watched Chippenham play three times. They were a very physically strong side but Keith and I both felt we had the necessary pace to get beyond their very rigid back four. After about an hour and a half we were boarding our coach to head back to our hotel and an evening meal.

Burnham Beeches was an absolutely beautiful place it had a huge wrap around manicured lawn. After dinner, everybody moved to the front of the hotel to sit on the grass and one of the many benches dotted around. It was a beautiful balmy May evening. I sat on a bench with my chairman. I asked him how things were going with the re-development.

He told me tactfully: "We are at an impasse", going on to say that his legal people had told him he was throwing good money after bad'. This wasn't good news for me as my contract with the club would be up on Monday.

So conceivably tomorrow could be my last game as manager of the club. What a way to go out!

It got to about 9:30 and because the evening was so warm, I had to encourage everyone to retire for perhaps one last cup of tea and then onto their rooms for a final bit of television.

Terry Martin came to me earlier that evening and said the players didn't want to know the team until as late as possible. I said that was fine and that I would announce it at tomorrow morning's last Team meeting. He passed the word around.

It must have been fairly obvious what my selection would be as I had named the same eleven for both semi-final legs and the quarter final. The only positions up for grabs were the substitutes, goalkeeper and centre forward.

Colin and I were rooming together and it was nearly midnight before we went to our room. It seemed we still had so much to talk about.

Our conversation went on when we got into bed. There were so many different arguments for either Lovell or Turner or Warden, Roberts or Ash, Lakin or Kempster, Tucker or Jamie Turner...

I woke about 7.15 am with the sun streaming through the window. I got out of bed to draw the curtains and while I was there I lifted the window and peered out.

Our room was on the second floor at the front of the hotel overlooking the beautiful manicured lawn where we had all been sitting that previous evening. It was already getting very hot.

Colin was awake as well, he sat up and said: "Close them fucking curtains, it's like Blackpool illuminations in here!".

I laughed and said: "Fuck the sunlight, feel the heat!".

I offered to make him a cup of tea whilst he got up to

look out of the window. "Bloody hell" he said, "that will be a leveller". He drank his tea while I took a shower.

When I got out and dried off I took a pre-arranged phone call from BBC Radio Kent. Since 1996 I had been their local football expert. I would go into the studio on a Friday evening to review all of the following day's football. I would often pop into the studio in midweek to pre -record interviews with guests of my choosing to air on the Friday night sports show.

Contrary to popular opinion I never received a penny from the BBC. I was just grateful to be a part of the local radio football scene. I worked alongside some legends of local radio sports. People like the late Neil Bell, Rob Smith, John Warnett and Matt Davison.

When the interview was done it was downstairs for a light breakfast, then I assembled the players in the room Burnham Beeches had set aside for us. I announced the team as well as the substitutes.

There were some small details to go over again. Keith, Colin and I had left no stone unturned.

Getting to Wembley was the easy bit. Winning was something completely different. The chairman popped his head round the door and asked to come in. He came to the front of the room to address the players. He thanked them for their achievement of reaching Wembley.

Roy was a very dogmatic individual and not one for showing his emotions but as he spoke to the players I detected a crack in his voice as he fought to hang on to that reserved exterior.

At about 11.30, my mobile rang, it was Steve Forrest to tell me that Emma had given birth to a daughter, Hannah. I congratulated him and asked him to give everyone's love and best wishes to her and the baby. May 6th 2000, a birthday I will never forget. All we had to do now was win!

FROM THE DEN TO WEMBLEY

Roy had arranged for the coach carrying all the friends and family to stop by the hotel at around 11:45pm to spend time with the guys before going off to play in this huge game. Again, there were lots and lots of photographs being taken.

The squad looked resplendent in their jet black suits, black shirts and black and white striped Deal town ties. The heat felt like it had ramped up a couple of degrees.

The next surprise was a police outrider who was going to lead the coach into Wembley. I gave him a Deal Town scarf and asked him mischievously to tie it on the rear of his bike. He was only too happy to oblige.

The friends and family coach set off, then it was our turn to make our way to the biggest game of our lives. So, with the police outrider leading the way, we pulled out of the hotel grounds and onto the A40 for the 20 minute drive to the "Venue of Legends". I sat down immediately behind the driver and beside me was ex-manager Dave Dadd.

Dave's involvement with the club went back many years. I half turned to him and said "Dave, I want you to lead the team out today" He looked at me and said: "Tom, I can't do that, it's my club but it's your team". That was typical of Dave, unselfish and very humble. As we reached the notorious Hangar Lane roundabout we glided through the lights courtesy of our police outrider holding back the traffic. It was exactly at this point we got our first view of the stadium about half a mile in the distance. There stood the twin towers gleaming in the fierce sunshine. I had to swallow hard as the realisation of what we were about to do in the next few hours hit home. Carrying on with our journey we pulled into the stadium car park where there were at least one hundred coaches decked out in Chippenham blue and white and Deal black and white. I knew that we had sold 8,000 tickets so between the both clubs there was going to be at least 20,000 people in attendance. The previous week Kingstonian had beaten Kettering 3-2 in the FA Trophy final in front of 20,034 fans. Could we top that I wondered?

We arrived at the two huge oak doors that we entered the previous day, only today there was no tour, it was down to business within an hour or so.

The heat was really oppressive as we filed into the right hand dressing room. We had a strict timetable: 2:40 on the pitch to warm up; 2:44 back in the dressing room; 2:52 line up in tunnel before entering the stadium; 2:53 introduction to guest of honour and various dignitaries; 2:56 the national anthem.

In our dressing room were two men in white coats wearing shirts and ties. They were there to assist us in any way they could. When we first entered our dressing room, there on a table was a box full of 100 matchday programmes. As you would expect there was a clamour to get at them.

I tried to intervene and limit each person to three programmes because I wanted to save some for the club. I tried to get the players to sit down and start to get them changed into their warm up gear.

It was 2:25 and we had 15 minutes to get on the pitch. I told Colin, who was going to take the warm-up, to keep it to an absolute minimum. The heat was now off the scale.

During the build up to Wembley, we had all had tattoos done on the top of our thighs. This was Colin's idea because after beating The Metropolitan Police back in the fifth round he made us promise we'd all get them done. Colin designed the tattoo and so one evening in the week before Wembley we all sat apprehensively in Kev's tattoo parlour in Welling High Street, waiting to be branded.

The Sun newspaper got wind of what was going on and sent photographers to record the moment. As a result we appeared the following Saturday in a centre page spread documenting our commitment to the cause.

With the players having followed Fordy on to the pitch, I got talking to the two guys in the white coats one told me he had been in the England dressing room that day in 1966.

I was gradually lowering my heartbeat talking with these two chaps. Eventually I made my way to the top of the tunnel, it was 2:34. I had resisted the temptation to put some kit on and join in the warm up.

I thought better of it because this was a day for the players, not some 46-year-old former player with only one good knee. I did however decide to have my moment regardless.

I was stood just inside the opening of the tunnel watching the guys go through their paces. To my right and around to the Royal Box it was a sea of black and white.

I gradually walked out of the tunnel.

Eventually, after a few seconds, the Deal fans recognised me and turning to applaud them I received an enormous ovation in return. I made my way back to the dressing room and, one-by-one the players followed me in. We had both had our moment.

There wasn't a lot of time to say much so while the players were putting their kit and boots on, I spoke about what we had to do and each individual's responsibilities. Whilst still speaking, the FA official knocked on the door to ask us to leave the dressing room. There was a lot of clapping and shouts of "Come on Boys!"

Terry stepped across me and led the players out into the bottom of the tunnel. I also stepped out into the tunnel. The first person I saw was Tommy Saunders. We shook hands and embraced one another warmly. The FA official Adrian Whiteson pushed Tommy and myself to the front of each group of players. Tommy had with him a young lad who was their mascot.

Our mascot was our chairman's daughter, 12-year-old Laura Smith but she was nowhere to be seen as we reached the mouth of the tunnel. Suddenly I felt a pull on my sleeve and there was Laura in full Deal Town kit. Mr Whiteson encouraged Tom and I to follow him as he walked out into the Wembley cauldron, it was hot and humid.

The noise was incredible, so as we picked our way over the wooden boards on top of the sand I told Laura to wave to everyone. Her late arrival in the tunnel meant all the nerves I had walking alongside her vanished. The MC on the Tannoy was screaming: "Please welcome Deal Town and Chippenham Town!"

As far as I knew this was going to be the last Vase final - or any other non-league final - for a number of years at this stadium which was to be demolished in the next few weeks to make way for a new Wembley. Reaching the halfway line we stopped and lined up to be introduced to the current chairman of the Football Association and other dignitaries. Our next obligation was to sing the national anthem. We had discussed this as a team and had decided to sing it with as much gusto as we could.

Once we'd finished I stepped out of line and turned right to shake my players' hands and say one last "Good luck". I couldn't believe it as I was going down the line, almost everyone was in tears. I couldn't blame them because I was super emotional as well.

My immediate thought was: "Hang about, we've got to play a game of football in the next few minutes". My last port of call was Terry Martin. I wished him well and he looked me in the eye saying: "Don't worry Tom, we'll be fine". If he said don't worry that was good enough for me.

As the day was so hot the officials were going to allow water breaks. I asked the fourth official if he knew the actual temperature. "That's no problem" he answered, and, pushing a miniature temperature gauge into the grass, he showed me: it read 33 degrees Celsius, just under 100 degrees Fahrenheit!

We kicked off and started very strongly forcing four corners in the first five minutes. Set pieces were going to be vital in the stifling conditions. Just before the game started I had said to Ribbo: "Don't worry about anything we've worked on, when you get your first throw, just throw it as far as you can!".

So when Paul got his first one he launched it right at Chippenham's far post where their 'keeper nicked it off of Steve Marshall's head. That throw must have been an adrenaline-fuelled 45 yards.

I just wanted to put the wind up Chippenham's defenders, just in case they hadn't been told. We had used this tactic sparingly in the build up to today, it's quite possible that anyone Tom had sent to see us couldn't have reported back on something he hadn't seen.

Then, after eleven minutes, disaster struck.

Left wing-back David Monteith, whilst chasing back, pulled up like he had been shot. Dave Dadd rushed on to see what he had done and came back and saying: "Knee ligaments". He said he wanted to give it five minutes, who could blame him I thought after all he had been through.

That five minutes Monty wanted turned out to be only three. When the ball came to him he tried controlling it before slumping into a heap on the pristine Wembley turf with one hand raised appealing for help.

Again, Dave Dadd rushed to his aid. Realising there was nothing he could do, he asked for a stretcher which the first aid people duly supplied. Seeing Monty being carried off the pitch left us all feeling sick to our stomachs.

They wheeled him around to right below the Royal Box. I rushed off from where I was sitting next to Keith, Colin and the subs. Five seconds later I was kneeling beside Monty, trying to learn the seriousness of his injury. Dave was in tears, not from pain but from knowing his big day was over. I could feel another presence beside me. It was his wife. She was as distraught as he was.

The first-aiders wanted to take him away to the hospital ward they had in the stadium where they could make him comfortable and examine him.

I was still in shock as they were taking my player away when I was spun around by Colin who shouted at me: "Come on, there's nothing you can do here, we've got a fucking game to win". It had been over five minutes since Dave had been carried off.

We had played all that time with ten men I now had to make my substitution. I looked at the bench and shouted to Paul Roberts: "Get stripped, you're going on".

Paul had missed out on starting the game only because my central-defender Jason Ash had proved himself fit in the previous weeks. Paul was also a central defender so I sent him on making three positional changes. I look back now realising that I was probably in shock at Monty's injury, because having sent Paul on we now had four central defenders in a back five.

In the last 15 minutes before the half time, Chippenham squandered two very good chances to take the lead. I breathed a huge sigh of relief when Football League referee David Laws blew his whistle for half time, we were lucky to still be in it at 0-0.

I cleared my mind and spoke to the players telling them to forget about Monty, there was nothing any of us could do about him now, but he doesn't want a runners up medal. I then undid the mess I had left the team in after I had sent Paul on.

I could see the first-half heat had taken its toll on Steve Lovell. He looked absolutely exhausted. I asked him if he could give me some more. "Yes" he replied instantly. Seconds later the buzzer sounded for us to return to the pitch.

As they all filed past me I shouted: "The last two Vase finals have been won in the dying minutes of the game". It was a statement that would prove prophetic...

I walked behind the players and out from the tunnel into the torturous heat. Sitting back down in my seat next to Keith my immediate concern was my veteran striker. Turning to Keith I said: "We'll get Lovell off soon."

We started the second half really strong. Getting back into a shape that suited us meant that we could follow instructions on how to deal with our opponent easier. The noise was deafening. I had to shout at Keith just to make myself heard I couldn't help but think about Monty and how was he feeling. I had a hunch that he'd had another ACL injury. The heat was bordering on dangerous.

There were at least 20 bottles of water in our goal, so every time there was a break in play at our end for a corner or a throw, the referee allowed the players to drink.

We were now about an hour into the game, so I decided it was time to give Steve Lovell a break. I told the fourth official we wanted to make our first substitution. He got his board ready with the number nine showing. In the last seven or eight games I had replaced Steve with Jonny Warden but on this occasion I sent Phil Turner on.

Phil was still buzzing from his Kent Senior Trophy Final hat-trick a fortnight ago. Phil was desperately unlucky not to have started the game. If I had known in advance how hot today was going to be I would have started him in front of Steve no question.

When Steve came off he received a fantastic ovation from both sets of supporters. Everybody knew that this was his last ever game in senior football. He deserved that ovation simply because of his exceptional career. I adored the man for the way he accepted playing at the lowest level of his career so far. Jon Warden was a bit bemused at not replacing Steve. I said to him this is looking like going to extra time so no problem if it does, you will play that final period. He nodded and said: "Thanks Gaffer".

We were now in the final twenty minutes and were forcing the issue so much so that Steve Marshall was hauled down in the penalty area by a Chippenham defender's clumsy challenge.

Time stood still as me and my staff and thousands of Deal Town fans waited for Mr Laws to signal for a penalty. No whistle was forthcoming and the game continued.

I looked at my watch and we had played 76 minutes. We were bossing the game now and in Marshall, Turner and Graham we carried a real goal threat.

I was very lucky to have in my side some very fit young players - especially a central-midfielder called Steve Best. When I say "young" I mean mid twenties. I had signed Steve back in my Herne Bay days as a 20 goal-a-season man. He was now a fantastic holding midfielder who was almost irreplaceable, and since losing Wayne Schweiso he had stepped up to become an inspiration to the rest of the team.

We had now played 82 minutes. It was plain that whoever scored next would hold the trophy aloft. Tommy Saunders was making his substitutions, sensing, like me, extra time was imminent.

On 85 minutes I was getting messages from the pitch that my central defender Jason Ash was not feeling well and was in danger of fainting.

I immediately summoned Jon Warden to get changed. Ash was a very fair headed lad and the heat just got the better of him. When he got to the touchline you could see how dizzy he was. I didn't make any positional changes, learning from the first half debacle. I told Jon to just put himself about a bit.

He did exactly that, winning some great headers in midfield and threatening Chippenham's two centre halves with his physicality.

We were now in the last nerve-shredding stages. On 86 minutes Marshall got away and only a brilliant last ditch tackle from Chippenham's captain and centre half Lee Burns prevented Steve from winning the game for us, but we did have a corner.

The Deal fans were in full voice now, sensing this could be our moment. Our regular corner taker Roly Graham slung in a disappointing inswinging kick which was caught easily by goalkeeper Ian Jones. He then proceeded to throw it to left back Shane Andrews who carried the ball slowly towards the halfway line. I was going ballistic shouting at Steve Best to shut him down.

In that instant Andrews rolled the ball forward to his central striker, where Jamie Kempster intercepted the ball and passed it forward to Steve Marshall on the halfway line. Marshy turned and set off for Chippenham's penalty area. He by-passed one defender's despairing attempt to tackle him and on he went towards the 18 yard box.

On the bench we were all on our feet waiting for him to cut in towards Chippenham's goal. Instead, he looked up to see both Roly Graham and Phil Turner completely unmarked in the heart of the penalty area. He then clipped this teasing little right-footed cross into the path of the onrushing Roly Graham. In that split second I shouted in my mind: "Hold it."

Roly though had other ideas as he struck the ball first time on the volley into the top corner of Ian Jones's net. Roly then went on the longest lap of honour in the history of great Wembley goals. I leapt high into the air as we all did on the bench. I considered jumping over the Carlsberg advertising hoarding about five yards in front of me but I thought better of it as I got closer. I looked up at the digital screen. It read: 87 minutes - Deal Town 1 Chippenham Town 0.

I was on cloud nine. Keith, Colin and I hugged each other at the same time as bouncing up and down. Then I clicked into pessimistic mode as I realised that there were still three minutes left and it was conceivable they could grab an equaliser. I needn't have worried.

When the full time whistle eventually blew, everyone raced forward to get onto the pitch and congratulate the players. I then did one of the things I am most proud of, I walked very calmly across the walkway that separated the two technical areas. I found Tommy Saunders sobbing his heart out. I kissed him on the top of his head and said to him: "Me and you are going to be friends for life". He looked up at me and tearfully said "Yes, thank you", and I have to say we still are close pals who talk regularly 23 years later.

The celebrations went on for at least 35 minutes after the game had finished. Another moment of great chivalry that day was when captain Terry Martin called the players over in front of all the Chippenham supporters to applaud them for the great support they had given their team. In return, the Chippenham fans saluted the victors. While all this was going on, David Monteith had returned just in time to see Roly score the winner.

Monty was on crutches and because of this Steve Best carried him up the stairs of the Royal Box to collect his medal. Terry was just about to lift the trophy to show the fans as I made my way up the stairs. I met Monty where he presented me with the cup. He looked at me and tearfully said: "You deserve that Boss".

I made my way back down the stairs to be confronted by Terry Martin. He looked at me and said: "That's it Tom, I'm packing up playing. I can't top this, I can't imagine playing in front of 320 people after today". He also felt that with his regular job taking up more of his time, now was as good a time as any to quit. While he was on a high.

After reminding him of the old adage that you are a long time retired, I went on to tell him what a great player he had been for me and that the door would always be open. We had one final embrace before a press man asked us both to follow him to the official press conference.

I heard someone call out "Dad!" and turned around to see my daughter Danielle walking towards me. My daughter and I had not seen each other for 18 months. I had split up with her mum many moons ago and sadly we had drifted apart. It was a very emotional reunion, and after a couple of minutes chatting together I was hurried along to the press conference where I found Terry and Roly fielding questions from local and national press outlets.

I sat down to answer my own questions. I was very friendly with some of the national non-league journalists, guys like Nick Harling, Walter Gammie and Colin Mafham.

They all had my phone number and I always gave them good value for money. After the predictable questions about how happy we were to be Wembley winners were out of the way, one asked me if it was true that my contract had run out and I would be leaving the club in the coming days.

I could only confirm that my contract did indeed run out the following day but that my future was in the hands of my Chairman and with that the conference broke up.

More than that I honestly didn't know. My future was actually in the hands of Dover District Council because if they didn't allow Roy to build the new stand facility, I could find myself out of a job.

The reception for the two teams was in a room directly behind the Royal Box. On the way there, Roly insisted I take a photo of him with the goal he scored the winner over his shoulder. I duly obliged.

Before we left Wembley I jumped on the Deal Town supporters coach which was about to leave to simply say thank you for their time and support. It was a very emotional few seconds and I happily posed for photos.

The press photographers took dozens of pictures of me, Roly and Terry.

Back at Burnham Beeches we had a wonderful celebration dinner. I said a few words, as did Roy. The hotel had laid on DJs to entertain the winning team and the room mercifully had patio doors leading to the beautifully manicured lawn as the heat had relented only slightly it was still very warm.

Where everybody believed we had a big knees-up of a party, it was actually a very calm and understated evening, simply because everyone was so tired. I can remember distinctly chatting to Steve Lovell and his lovely wife Mary in the early hours of the morning in shorts and shirtsleeves.

A fantastic end to a fantastic day.

FROM THE DEN TO WEMBLEY

Deal public turn out in force

Deal Town FC Wembley team

FROM THE DEN TO WEMBLEY

Jamie Kempster celebrates after giving us an early lead against Mossley

Keith Lissenden - Assistant Manager's right hand man

Dave Dadd - Turned down the opportunity to lead the team out.

Colin Ford - life long friend and first team coach

FROM THE DEN TO WEMBLEY

Deal Town singing the National Anthem - proudest moment of my career

On the Wembley tour - I'm in the back row at the end on the right.

Team on the lawn of Burnham Beeches suited and booted

FROM THE DEN TO WEMBLEY

Leading my team out with 12 year old mascot Laura Smith (chairman's daughter)

Expectant father - Steve Forrest

One of the iconic twin towers - breathtaking sight

FROM THE DEN TO WEMBLEY

Dave Monteith - Dave's Wembley final over after 11 minutes

Match-winner Roly Graham on the ball

FROM THE DEN TO WEMBLEY

The winning goal

Winner

Phil Turner - wish list player

Jon Warden lapping up the occasion

FROM THE DEN TO WEMBLEY

Celebrations in the Royal box

Me relaxing with the trophy, 24 hours later - all the hard work done.

11
WHAT HAPPENED NEXT?

During the evening The chairman pulled me aside to inform me that my contract would not be renewed because Dover District Council had not offered the lease he wanted.

I still can't believe it to this day. Roy had pledged £750,000 of his own money to build a facility that the whole of the town's community could benefit from. Roy's legal people advised him to pull out of any more negotiations.

Whilst I was devastated to hear this news on my greatest ever day in football, I could understand Roy's reasoning. Here I was at a Kent League club on the equivalent of £850 per week gross and an £80,000 per season budget. It was never going to be affordable going forward. The official attendance for the final was 20,085 from which Deal took £75,000 after corporation tax.

I decided to not tell anybody, but would address the players at breakfast. Of course with Roy stepping away from the club this meant the players would all be released. I got on the phone to my good friend Stuart Hammonds who reported for the non-league paper. This would need even more publicity that weekend because I couldn't afford to be out of the game for too long!

Roy had handed me an envelope just after our conversation. I opened it in private and it once again confirmed my opinion of Roy being a generous man.

The following morning I gathered the players around me to tell them of the situation. It was a very emotional meeting. Me and the team I had built were going our separate ways.

The next week saw us all in limbo. I was getting phone calls from managers all around Kent asking for players' phone numbers. It was a painful process for me. Knowing that the guys I had been so close to for nearly a decade were going to play for someone else.

The ensuing publicity around my leaving the club meant that my phone was red hot that coming week.

Dulwich Hamlet and Boreham Wood wanted to speak to me first. I spoke to Dulwich and decided to say no after I was offered the job. Next up was an offer to take over at Isthmian Premier League side Boreham Wood.

I had heard on the grapevine that their chairman Danny Hunter was a nightmare to work for, having gone through six managers in the previous eight months, I suppose the writing was on the wall early on, yet I agreed to take over in October 2000.

My first game was away to Croydon and it couldn't have gone any better, winning 5-0.

I received a congratulations phone call that evening from a very good friend of mine, Ex-apprentice colleague at Millwall, George Borg, now manager at league leaders Aldershot Town. George told me: "Tom, you've taken on a whole lot of grief there." but I assured George I could handle it.

The following Saturday was my first home league game in charge. Our opponents Hampton and Richmond Borough were much stronger opponents than last week's strugglers Croydon. This was going to be a severe test for me. I had only been in the club one week and had just two training sessions to try and introduce the 3-5-2 formation that I preferred.

The Hampton game went like a dream, winning 3-2 in an exciting end-to-end match and two wins on the bounce left me rubbing my hands together. It had been a terrific start and I had introduced myself as a winner, but that bubble soon burst as a midweek visit to Basingstoke saw us beaten 0-1 in the last few minutes.

I wasn't at all perturbed. Our next game was an FA Trophy game at Purfleet. Facing me in that game were two ex-Deal Town players in Steve Marshall and Martin Buglione. Both Marshy and Bugsy got on the scoresheet for our hosts in a worrying 2-4 defeat. The chairman was getting into the players' ears about this new formation the new manager was trying and failing to introduce productively.

The following training night I sat the players down and told them, in no uncertain terms, to get used to this system or fuck off and play for someone else. Our next league game was at home to Hitchin Town. We were cruising 2-0 up late in the game before Hitchin scored a very late consolation goal.

Three wins out of four was, I thought, a decent return for a new manager trying to stamp his mark on his new team.

My next game was at my old mate George Borg's Aldershot who were flying at the top of the league and playing in front of huge crowds. We were comfortably in the top half of the table and showing as good a form as anyone in the league.

After going through some last minute details I left the away team dressing room with my teamsheet in hand to visit the referee's room, shutting the door behind me, I bumped into the chairman.

He held his hand out and said: "Let me have a look at your team".

I gave him the team sheet to look at and, after glancing through it, he said: "What formation are you playing"?

"3-5-2" I replied curtly.

Frowning, he came straight back at me: "You can't play that system here you'll get slaughtered. I advise you to change it".

The red mist descended. "Give me that sheet back, I'm late to see the referee" I fumed.

"Don't say I didn't warn you" he responded calmly, handing it back to me.

Seething, I knocked on the referee's door and went in. I returned to my dressing room to give the players one last 'good luck', and shook hands with everybody as they filed past me into the watery November sunshine. I sat down in my dugout before getting up to shake George Borg's outstretched hand. "Have a good one" we both said together.

The game kicked off and as expected we had to weather a very early storm. My system was built to soak up pressure and catch our opponents on the break. Exactly the way my Deal Town team had won the Vase five months ago. We came in at half-time 1-0 up through youngster Steve Sinclair's goal. I sensed the players were warming to the way we were playing, especially the more senior players.

The second half panned out the way the first half had. Pressure and break-aways. We stunned the 2,000 Aldershot fans when late substitute Brian Jones added our second goal to win 2-0. I felt fully redeemed that I had ignored Hunter's warning about my system.

The dressing room was rightly cock-a-hoop after an absolutely fantastic result. The door opened and the chairman walked in with a beaming smile all over his face. He shook my hand, saying: "Well done Tom".

I couldn't help thinking: 'you fucking two faced bastard!'. Danny beckoned to me as he walked to the door. I followed him upstairs until we reached the Aldershot boardroom. He then started to introduce his new manager to the officials of our hosts. He was gushing about 'what a great appointment he had made'. I shook hands with one man who said to me in front of Danny: "Congratulations on winning the Vase."

I got into my car feeling ecstatic, but also very wary of Hunter. I had just spent two years with an absolute gentleman of a chairman in Roy Smith and now I was working for a man who I couldn't trust as far as I could throw him!

The following Tuesday we had a Hertfordshire County Cup match against a local County League side. I was tempted to rest players after their exertions the previous Saturday but I decided against it although I knew this coming Saturdays match at home to Kingstonian would be tough.

A 2-0 win in the County Cup match saw my record extend to six wins from seven. The following Thursday the chairman called a players meeting. I had my feet firmly under the table now and was starting to feel more comfortable around the place. I was disappointed with the apathy of our supporters. We were struggling to get 180 people through the turnstiles and when we did play at home the atmosphere was like the wake of a person nobody liked.

I sat in on the chairman's meeting and looked on in amazement as he picked out certain players and started to fine them for bad tackles he felt they had gotten away with in recent games. The players tried to argue with his decisions but he refused to budge. Amounts of £50 and £40 were bandied about.

As Hunter ranted on, players were looking at me as if I knew this was going to happen. I just kept shrugging my shoulders.

I did try to intervene but he shut me up saying: "This has got nothing to do with you".

I responded with: "I'm the manager and these are my players" but it fell on deaf ears.

The meeting ended and as he left the room the players were in uproar. I promised to see what I could do. We had already lost an hour of a training night so I decided to park the issue for the time being and get on with some work.

Because the Arsenal Ladies team used the pitch on Sundays we were severely limited as to when we could use it. There were however two tarmac tennis courts alongside the car park, so, most training nights I had to improvise, playing games of head tennis. This meant we could do very little meaningful work. I felt I was banging my head against a very large brick wall.

One evening after I arrived home from training, I had an answerphone message from a guy called Cliff Hercules who was the manager at Aylesbury. Cliff asked me could I ring him back. I didn't know him very well other than having played against him in my early Dartford days. I contacted him the following day and he asked me if I knew that my chairman had been phoning around clubs offering them my striker John Lawford and centre-half Gary Wotton.

I didn't have a clue.

I phoned Hunter to tackle him about this revelation. He was obviously taken aback by the fact I knew this. He mumbled his apologies, saying these players being 'bad eggs' and he wanted them out of his club. I told him that I was the manager and any decision on players coming or going would be down to me'. I also added that if I found out he had phoned another club about footballing matters I would be off.

It wasn't long before I found out that he had called Hendon's manager Dave Anderson about getting rid of my goalkeeper!

This was all becoming too much. I phoned the chairman and ripped into him: "If you wanted to be the manager why the fuck did you employ me?" He mumbled his apologies before I slammed the phone down on him.

I was starting to feel desperate about things. I had been used to having total control and here I was being undermined at every turn. I think Hunter thought that he could manipulate me and get his own way. I had been in the club about a month and my results had been excellent, but not being allowed on the pitch to work constructively was getting me down and thoughts about resigning were never far away.

The following week we were at home to Kingstonian and got torn apart by a very good, well organised team, losing 1-3. The morale in the dressing room was non-existent. I kept asking myself: should I stay and try and regain control?

The next morning I got a call from a very old friend of mine, Ben Embery the manager of Braintree, to say my chairman has been on the phone asking how much did he want for their striker. I explained I'd been having trouble with Hunter about this kind of interference. It was the last straw and I made my mind up I was going to resign after the next training session.

I called George Borg and told him of my predicament. I could tell straight away that he understood: "You are better off out of it Tom, you'll always get another job".

Speaking to George made me feel better about my decision. I had taken an impossible job and I shouldn't reproach myself in any way. I decided not to give Hunter advanced warning of my decision. He was almost always there on training nights so I thought I would go as normal and tell him before or afterwards.

When I got there that following Tuesday evening I saw his car parked up. I decided not to go into the dressing room. I wanted to speak to him. I walked into his office and sat down opposite him.

I started by saying: "OK you've won. I've had enough of your constant interference. This has worn me down to the point where I am going to resign as of now."

The next few seconds were surreal as, when I got up to leave the office, he followed me out into a deserted bar. He was begging me not to leave saying: "If you go you will make me a laughing stock of the league".

I looked at him and said I really didn't care. I started to turn towards the door and as I did, he dropped down to his knees in front of me and, putting his arms around my waist, kept begging me not to leave. I felt very uncomfortable at all this and I finally extricated myself from his grasp.

The whole scene was excruciatingly embarrassing. I finally made it to the door with him still on his knees, and with a "Good luck for the season..." got in my car and drove out of the ground feeling very awkward at the whole turn of events.

The journey home took about an hour and a half and in that time I had three or four players call me having heard what had happened, all saying how disappointed they were that I had left the club!

They all said how much they had enjoyed playing for me. I was touched by that sentiment. In truth we had not really scratched the surface, because of the lack of time spent training on the pitch. I was feeling very relieved and it felt that a huge weight had been lifted from my shoulders.

I telephoned Stuart Hammonds from the non-league paper to tell him of my situation and ask him for a bit of publicity over the coming weekend so that I could get my name out there again.

My phone was on fire with players ringing me. A couple of the more experienced ones told me they recognised how difficult it must have been working with Hunter. It only made me feel more vindicated in my decision to leave. I had been at the club five weeks and won five out of six games, winning 15 points in the process. Having started the job with the club in mid-table, I left them in fifth place.

Boreham Wood are now a well established National League club so I take my hat off to Danny Hunter and his club's achievement. I was the right manager at the wrong time for them. He probably thought just because I had come out of the Kent League he could bully me. Well, we saw how that worked out didn't we!

When the dust settled and people found out I was available, I got phone calls from Dover Athletic and Dartford. Because of my attachment to Dartford, having played over 200 games there, I agreed to talk to them.

The Darts were struggling in the Doc Martens Eastern Division and were ground sharing with Kent rivals Gravesend and Northfleet. The budget was a poor £1,200 per week and as manager I would receive £500 per month. It was a far cry from my days at Herne Bay and Deal and even Boreham Wood. But for the first time in my career I allowed sentiment to sway my decision.

I accepted Dartford's offer to become manager knowing that it was to be a huge task to move the club forward. The club's finances were in a parlous state. Attendances were very poor because Gravesend were seen as the deadly enemy and fans didn't want to watch their club play at their rival's stadium where they were paying an astronomical rent for the use of their facility.

The Eastern Division was very strong with several clubs working on a full time basis, such as Histon, Salisbury, Dorchester and Eastleigh.

Due to my history with Dartford I went in with a big reputation as a winner and was looked upon as a messiah-like figure. We had to train at a local university which had a full size redgrass surface. Exactly like the one I used to train on at Millwall all those years ago.

We were now into the new year 2001. My first game was away to Stamford where we narrowly lost 1-2 late on. The game highlighted two major factors: our fitness levels and lack of experience, which I immediately set about changing. We were in a league which in all honesty we couldn't handle.

I watched the under 18s youth team every Sunday morning without fail to see if there were any gems I could promote to the first team. There were in fact a couple of youngsters who impressed me but I would have to give them first team experience gradually.

I stayed with Dartford for four seasons, fighting like mad not to get relegated. I put as much into those survival seasons as I could, despite having a very inexperienced side. The supporters expected far too much. I took the brunt of their frustrations. At any one time I would be filling my team with four or five teenagers. I remember going to play at Dorchester who were top of the league and playing in a brand new stadium. I remember starting my teamtalk by looking around the dressing room at all these young faces and I began singing 'Baa baa black sheep have you any wool...'.

My first-team coach was a great guy called Paul Sawyer who, like me, had played well over 100 games for the club. He put his hands over his eyes: "What the fuck are you doing?"

"I'm trying to make them feel at home" I said

"You're off your trolley!" he replied, shaking his head.

As the players filed out the door to go and play the best team in the league, I explained: "Look, they are all giggling. I have taken away the fear of our opposition because I have taken their minds off of them".

Paul laughed and said: "Yep I make you right there, even I'm not worried anymore".

That summed me up my style of management, it always carried a bit of humour. I did my best for The Darts, achieving mid-table finishes against all the odds. My last season at the club was 2004/2005. Right to the end it was a terrible struggle. I had to blood many teenagers that season and we were struggling to keep our heads above the water. No matter what the result home or away I would always go into the bar to face the supporters, despite what may have been a heavy loss. I took all the flak that came my way.

One day after an away game at Uxbridge Town, the supporters took it out on the chairman and a couple of directors. The following Sunday morning I was watching the youth team playing when the chairman, an immensely likeable man called Dave Skinner, sidled up to my side. Without looking at me he said:

"Tom, can you attend a board meeting tomorrow night?"

In recent weeks the club had announced that it would be moving into a new stadium next season in Dartford.

I looked at him.

"You're going to fire me, aren't you?" I replied.

He looked me straight in the eyes and said: "Look, whatever happens, I promise you will still be the manager when we open the new stadium next season."

I attended the board meeting the following evening with my letter of resignation in my jacket pocket . At the meeting I heard all the same old crap, expecting the worst: "We thank you for all your hard work and your professionalism in what has been a very difficult time for the club" and left the meeting with them voting on my future. I told the chairman I would ring him in the morning for the result of the vote and when I called, he opened by saying: "Sorry Tom" and I knew the rest.

Before he could continue I said: "Dave, Dartford are not sacking me because I am coming round to you this morning with my letter of resignation".

"Fine" he said solemnly, "I will tell the board".

The next few days I was very down. I had asked to visit the players at training to say goodbye. It was very emotional for me as I had invested a lot of time and patience in some of these guys.

The reality of not being in the game for the first time in 31 years was a hard pill to swallow. I didn't go to a game for the rest of that season. I just wanted to avoid all those questions about 'What happened at Dartford?'

I did receive telephone calls from clubs that had a manager in place. I gave those types of calls short shrift as I was uncomfortable talking with clubs in those circumstances.

It was difficult being out of work as my life in the game was geared around Tuesdays, Thursdays and Saturdays. I had a dear old friend of mine who was the manager of Horsham YMCA in the Sussex County Premier League, John Suter. John and I met when my Herne Bay team played his Horsham side in the FA. Cup in the early 90s.

John and I remained good friends after that encounter and often spoke on the phone. He had been manager at YMCA for over 20 years and in the non-league world that longevity had to be respected.

At the end of the season after I left Dartford, John invited me to a game of his. It was the last day of the season for his team and if he won they would win the league.

I duly accepted and it was heartening to see John lift the trophy after beating Hassocks comfortably.

I had become a recluse where football was concerned. I enjoyed watching this game immensely because nobody knew me and I wasn't going to get interrogated about what happened at Dartford. It was great to celebrate with John. I met some of his players and it was nice to be around footballers after all this time.

That close-season was a very long and depressing one for me. I missed the general business of trying to sign players and organising pre-season training. I was now desperate to get back in to the game somewhere. Anywhere.

When John and I next spoke he asked me would I like to join him as first team coach. I jumped at the chance to help him despite the fact I lived in Maidstone now. It was 43 miles to Horsham - about a 45 minute drive. I accepted John's offer over the phone and I could hear in his voice how delighted he was.

Pre-season was to start in ten days. John asked me to meet him at the club to meet the players and do a press interview for the local rag. He introduced me to the players, many of which I had met a few weeks ago when they had become league champions.

The target for this coming season was to win the title again and gain automatic promotion to the Isthmian League Division One South. I told the players that I wasn't here to change them but to improve them.

I couldn't wait for pre-season to start. I wasn't a snob when it came to what level I was working in now. I sat with John after the players had left and he sheepishly asked me what money I would like to be paid.

I just told him to give me a tenner every now and then towards my petrol. He looked at me and said: "Are you sure?" telling me that the players got £20 per week regardless if they have played midweek or not.

I was amazed by this, because every where I had been involved in would never have played players for next to nothing as they were here.

When pre-season did start John gave me total control of what and how we did it. Those first two weeks saw me get to know the players. I also laid my own little piece of law down. Players were inclined to call me "Mate". I told them I wasn't their mate, but Gaffer or Tom would do.

John stayed in the background those first few weeks. I was happy for him to deal with players about travel arrangements to games and so on.

I had complete control at training. When the season started I always called John "Boss", so there was no distinction between him and me. I would always let John speak first in the dressing room before games.

I would then follow him with mainly details concerning what we might have worked on in training.

The order of dressing room hierarchy soon became clear to the players. I was enjoying myself working with these players and under John. He was delighted with the way it was working out. I was just so grateful to be working again.

By Christmas we were right in the mix and that first few months had me enjoying myself for the first time since those early years at Sheppey and Herne Bay. I never looked for Dartford's results, I was so happy to be involved at this wonderful little club.

The Chairman was a man called Mick Browning, who himself had been a top non-league goalscorer with the likes of Crawley, Tooting & Mitcham and even his country.

We eventually won the league and with nearly £35,000 being spent on the ground grading process we won promotion to the Isthmian League South East Division. This was a huge step up for the club and I realised because of my past experience I would have to take a lot on my shoulders. This was going to be a hugely challenging season.

This was the highest level of football the club had ever participated in. This applied to most of the players as well. Our first game away to Cray Wanderers was on a sizzling hot August Saturday afternoon.

We lost to a very late goal from legendary non-league striker Gary Abbott, but there was still much to be taken from it. I was delighted with the way we had played.

Our next fixture was the following Tuesday at home to Steve Lovell's Sittingbourne. We were 3-1 to the good with 15 minutes to go but with two horrendous blunders from our reserve team stopper in those final few minutes, we had to be satisfied with a point.

It was great to see Steve for the first time since Wembley. After our first two games and just with a point under our belt I felt we had enough to be a surprise package. I made the players understand that because we are 'little Horsham YMCA' many of the teams we would play against wouldn't take us seriously and that would be our trump card.

By mid-season we were in the top half of the table and holding our own. I have to confess I had never enjoyed my football as I had here. I enjoyed working with this group of players as much as I had with my players at Sheppey, Herne Bay and Deal.

I was getting used to being the underdog and thoroughly enjoying the tag. The players were getting used to my training methods and taking on board the amount of detail I was giving them each game.

John was happy to take a backseat and our partnership was working out even better than we both thought at the start of it. As each week went by we would find ourselves hovering about eighth in the table just outside the play-off positions. Every time we won I would follow the guys into the dressing room shouting: "The play-offs boys!".

I would look at John shaking his head and with this beaming smile and say: "Come on guv'nor, we can do it, Isthmian Premier League here we come!".

We would catch up in the bar and he would say: "Have you always been like this?"

"Yes" I would reply, "Always. To infinity and beyond as Buzz Lightyear would say!"

We would both laugh at the prospect of little old Horsham YMCA being an Isthmian League Premier club.

As the season drew to a close we had two games left away to Maidstone United and Fleet Town managed by ex-England international Andy Sinton. If we achieved maximum points it was likely we would finish in a play-off spot. Luckily for John, and probably the club, we lost both narrowly by a single goal. I was so disappointed, but looking at the club's new-found status the season had to be viewed as a success.

During pre-season I had a number of calls from clubs far and wide. The most intriguing was from Redhill FC. Their director of football Martin Larkin asked me to consider accepting the vacant manager's position.

Redhill, despite being in Surrey, competed in the Sussex County Premier Division, where I had extensive experience from my time at YMCA. He painted this picture of an ambitious club with a decent budget, planning to build a high-end training facility.

When I spoke to the Redhill board they confirmed the picture that Martin had painted, so I thought 'what the heck', this was a win-win situation and I agreed to take up the reins on a very acceptable salary. I asked my dear friend and ex-Bromley manager Stuart McIntyre to be my first team coach.

Stuart was a quality coach in his own right and I felt the two of us together would make an impressive management duo. I had already won the Sussex Premier League at Horsham YMCA, so I knew what we would be up against.

It was a wrench leaving Horsham but staying there and not taking Redhill would have been based on sentiment. I informed John of my decision and he accepted it with good grace. So July 2007 saw us start pre-season. I had brought in a couple of young lads from Dartford and we invited everyone from last year's Redhill team back, so for the next month Stuart and I were trying to sort out the wheat from the chaff.

Trying to assess players from last season as well as my players made for an extremely difficult pre-season. It was chaotic because nobody at the club had organised any friendlies, so Stuart and I had to call in a few favours and get some very last minute matches. One or two of last year's players had caught our eye and we started our season with an impressive 3-1 win over Eastbourne Town.

We followed that up with a couple of away draws. Five points from three games wasn't exactly championship winning form but I wasn't really concerned because all I could think about was another crack at the Vase.

Unfortunately, I never got that chance as something far bigger than the footballing fates took over.

While at home in early December 2007 I collapsed in my Kitchen. I managed to crawl on all fours to our bedroom where I collapsed on the bed in a daze. My wife Sandie came home and found me in a deep sleep. She woke me gently and as I stood up she could see that something was dreadfully wrong. I couldn't see straight, everything was blurred. I then followed her down the stairs, hanging on to the rail for fear of falling. When I got downstairs and into an armchair Sandie called for an Ambulance.

When they arrived an hour later I was rushed to Maidstone Hospital where I was diagnosed as having had a massive stroke.

Within about twelve hours I had lost the use of my left side completely. I also had trouble speaking, and my eyesight was blurred. I spent three weeks in hospital. I was desperate to know from my doctors what this meant for my future and I could sense their reluctance to tell me the truth. It was Sandie that confirmed that I had a long hard road in front of me.

I was 54 years of age and so I thought, as fit as a butcher's dog. I slowly realised that this was the end of my football career and my golf, my two passions as well as my social life. Sandie had run a health and social care business so fully understood the implications of this condition. Seven days-a-week care and round the clock observations. After leaving Maidstone Hospital I was transferred to the Wellington Hospital in St Johns Wood, London which dealt solely with brain injuries.

The facilities there were second-to-none. I was fortunate to have private medical insurance and took full advantage of it. The stroke had not only affected me but my wife, my brothers, my sister and everybody was poleaxed at my condition.

My elder brother Tony and I had played golf together once a week for nearly thirty years. In my dreams I would ask for one more round with Tony. Sadly that was never going to happen. When I eventually got home from being hospitalised it was September 2008, nine months after being struck down.

I had to officially resign from my job at Redhill and all forms of football.

When I came home I hit a wall of depression that left me despairing of what the future held for me. I consoled myself by spending a couple of years writing a book about my stroke experience, called 'Sudden Exit'. The title says it all. In the space of three seconds I lost everything. My golf, my football, my social life and my self esteem.

So there you have it, as far and me and football was concerned, this was the end.

But my story hasn't ended yet. If you've been paying attention, you should know me better than that!

I'm still fighting for the best possible life, with my wife Sandie right beside me.

I have to give a special mention to my Dear friend Steve Lovell who visited me regularly, despite his heavy workload at Gillingham FC. People like Steve and Alan Walker - who kindly wrote my foreword and last word - understand my pain because Steve's father Alan died not long after he suffered a stroke, whilst Walks suffered a broken neck in a freak accident while coaching in Ireland.

Words are cheap in this life. It's deeds that carry weight. Friends as a word doesn't tell the whole story where Alan and Steve are concerned. I will fight on regardless.

"Come on you Lions!"

FROM THE DEN TO WEMBLEY

FROM THE DEN TO WEMBLEY

THE LAST WORD

STEVE LOVELL

Football brought Tom and I together as friends many years ago. We had shared interests in not only football, but golf as well, and over the years we had countless conversations about teams and team selections on the golf course.

Tom has had a great career as a player and manager at many good football clubs with his greatest achievement coming in 2000 where he managed Deal Town to a 1-0 win in the FA Vase at the original Wembley Stadium which I had the privilege to play in.

After the shock of suffering a massive stroke in 2007, Tom has battled to come to terms with his condition, and he has been brilliant in the way he has adapted.

His wife Sandie has been a rock for him, and they are making the best of what is put before them. I am very proud of the way he has managed his life. Tom and I still speak regularly on the phone, mostly about my football exploits.

Tom's football achievements are well known throughout the non-league game and will never be forgotten.

This book is all about a man who has had great days and some very bad days but who has never given up, no matter what has been put before him.

I am very proud of Tom and always will be.

Steve Lovell

FROM THE DEN TO WEMBLEY

IN MEMORIAM

This book acknowledges those who played a part in my journey and sadly are no longer with us:

John Flaherty	Roger Bowen	Larry O'Connell
Alan Ballard	Graham Peacock	Martyn Taylor
Harry Cripps	Charlie Vaughan	George Cornes
Alf Wood	Martin Ford	Kenny Edwards
Barry Kitchener	Theo Foley	Glyn Beverly
Billy Holmes	Paul Foley	John Fiorini
Benny Fenton	Hughie Stinson	Vera Roberts
Lawrie Leslie	Harry Richardson	Bill Roberts
Barry Salvage	Andy Bushell	Colin Adams
Jeff Fulton	Keith Weller	Pam Adams
Jack Blackman	Joe Hodgkinson	Martin Collins
Brian Brown	Mike Browning	Andy Balentyne
Carole Sampson	Larry Kelly	Maisie Sampson
Johnny Sampson	Bob Snow	Jack Payne
Paul Sykes	Martin Taylor	Ernie Morgan
Charlie Greyhurst	Dave Tozer	Peter Wager
John Moules	Martin Taylor	Colin Boswell
Dave Jackson	Roy Vinter	Charlie Prior

Also available from Victor Publishing....

A SEASON TO REMEMBER
MILLWALL FC 1964/65
A Match by Match account of Millwall Football Club's 1964/65 Division Four Promotion Season

A SEASON TO REMEMBER
MILLWALL FC 1965/66
A Match by Match account of Millwall Football Club's 1965/66 Division Three Promotion Season

A SEASON TO REMEMBER
MILLWALL FC 1971/72
A match by match account of Millwall Football Club's famous 1971/72 'near miss' promotion season

A SEASON TO REMEMBER
MILLWALL FC 1975/76
A Match by Match account of Millwall Football Club's 1975/76 Division Three Promotion Season

A SEASON TO REMEMBER
MILLWALL FC 1984/85
A match by match account of Millwall Football Club's 1984/85 Division Three promotion season

A SEASON TO REMEMBER
MILLWALL FC 1987/88
A match by match account of Millwall Football Club's 1987/88 Division Two title-winning season

A SEASON TO REMEMBER
MILLWALL FC 1988/89
A match by match account of Millwall Football Club's 1988/89 Division One debut season

with NEIL FISSLER

Millwall Who's Who

A Complete Record of every player to represent Millwall FC

This essential publication for Millwall fans profiles every player who made a first-team appearance for the club since their first competitive game in 1886. Have you ever wondered what happened to all those players you have seen come and go over the years? The heroes and villains, the saints and sinners, the stars you have talked about for years after they retired and those who you instantly forgot.

**Available at:
www.victorpublishing.co.uk/shop
also available in paperback and Kindle
format at:
amazon**

Also available...

**30 - Millwall's
Three Decades at The Den**

**Daydreams &
Nightmares Millwall FC
in the 2000s Part 1**

**South Bermondsey
Homesick Blues - Millwall
FC in the 1990s Part 2**

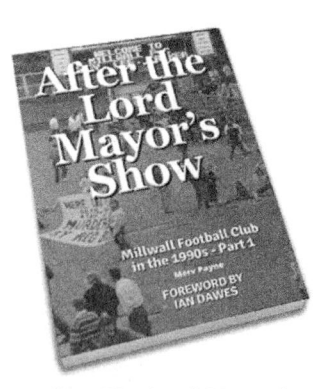

**After The Lord Mayor's
Show - Millwall FC in the
1990s Part 1**

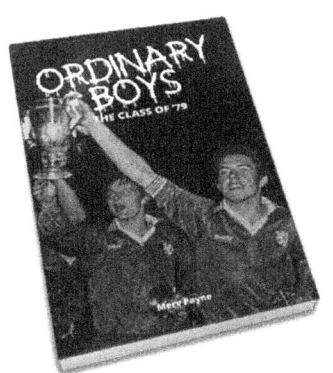

Ordinary Boys - The Class of '79 The Story of Millwall's FA Youth Cup Winning Heroes

A Natural High - Millwall FC's Two Seasons in the First Division

Because My Dad Does - Me, Dad & Millwall

Available at:
www.victorpublishing.co.uk/shop
also available in paperback and Kindle format at:

amazon

Also available...

The 1980s are remembered as a bleak time in the history of English football. Dismissed as a time the game was blighted by hooliganism and tragedy.

Since the advent of the Premier League in 1992, it's easy to forget that going to the match before then was still a hugely enjoyable experience, accessible and affordable to all.

With new, modern, often soulless, identikit stadiums now commonplace, also forgotten are the unique stands, terraces, facades and features that gave every club its own identity. This book unearths a huge, previously unseen treasure trove of images from that forgotten era.

An era that was, until now, lost.

Also available...

The Non-league Groundhopper's Diary is a fascinating journey around some of the country's most unique footballing homes.

Alan Burge's three volumes of travels takes in the spectacular, bizarre and long-forgotten world that still exists in the game's lower reaches of the footballing pyramid.

Together with his own thoughts and comments - and all-important reviews of the refreshments services - there are hundreds of fascinating football homes to explore, including incredible drone photography and also a section on stadiums that are no longer in use.

**Available at:
www.victorpublishing.co.uk/shop
also available in paperback and Kindle
format at:
amazon**

Got a book in you?

Victor Publishing
victorpublishing.co.uk

This book is published by Victor Publishing.

Victor Publishing specialises in getting new and independent writers' work published worldwide in both paperback and Kindle format.

If you have a manuscript for a book of any genre (fiction, non-fiction, autobiographical, biographical or even reference or photographic/illustrative) and would like more information on how you can get your work published and on sale to the general public, please visit us at:

www.victorpublishing.co.uk

victorpublishing.co.uk

Printed in Great Britain
by Amazon